AUGUST CRULL

and the Story of the Evangelical Lutheran Hymn-Book (1912)

JON D. VIEKER

Lutheran University Press
Minneapolis, Minnesota

AUGUST CRULL
and the Story of the
Evangelical Lutheran Hymn-Book (1912)

By Jon D. Vieker

Copyright © 2013 Jon D. Vieker. All rights reserved. Published by Lutheran University Press, an imprint of 1517 Media. No part of this book may be reproduced or transmitted in any form by any means, electronic, mechanical, recording, or otherwise, without the express permission of the publisher. For information or permission for reprints or excerpts, please contact the publisher.

Published under the auspices of:
   Center for Church Music
   Concordia University Chicago
   River Forest, IL 60305-1402

ISBN 978-1-932688-88-7
eISBN 978-1-942304-42-5

Contents

Abbreviations...4

Introduction 5

C. F. W. Walther and *KELG* 1847 7

KELG 1847 and Transitional English-Language Hymnals 11

ELHB 1889 and Hymnals from Other Lutheran Churches 17

The Life and Times of August Crull 26

August Crull as Editor of *ELHB* 1889......................33

The Long Journey toward *ELHB* 1912 51

The Sluggish Arrival of *ELHB* 1912 60

Conclusion...70

Appendix One: German-Language Hymns
from Pre-*ELHB* 1889 Collections 72

Appendix Two: English-Language Hymns
from Non-Missouri Synod Hymnals 76

Appendix Three: Comparison of Thematic Headings
in *KELG* 1847 and *ELHB* 1889............................84

Missouri Synod Hymnals and Sunday School Hymnals..........86

Abbreviations

BoW 1870	*Book of Worship*, General Synod, 1870.
CB 1868	*Church Book for the Use of Evangelical Lutheran Congregations*, General Council, 1868.
DH 1879	*Hymn Book for the Use of Evangelical Lutheran Schools and Congregations* [Decorah Hymnal], Norwegian Synod, 1879.
ELH 1880	*Evangelical Lutheran Hymnal*, Ohio Synod, 1880.
ELHB 1889	*Evangelical Lutheran Hymn Book*, English Synod, 1889.
ELHB 1892	*Evangelical Lutheran Hymn-Book*, English Synod, 1892.
ELHB 1912	*Evangelical Lutheran Hymn-Book*, Missouri Synod, 1912.
KELG 1847	*Kirchengesangbuch für Evangelisch-Lutherische Gemeinden ungeänderter Augsburgischer Confession*, Missouri Synod, 1847.
SSH 1901	*Sunday-School Hymnal*, English Synod, 1901.

Introduction

This study is based on a chapter from a forthcoming Ph.D. dissertation in Historical Theology from Concordia Seminary, St. Louis, titled: "The Fathers' Faith, the Children's Song: Missouri Lutheranism Encounters American Evangelicalism in Its Hymnals and Hymns, 1889–1912." Portions of this study previously appeared in "August Crull and His Legacy as Lutheran Hymnal Editor and Translator," CrossAccent: The Journal of the Association of Lutheran Church Musicians *16, no. 3 (2008): 39–51. Special thanks to Concordia Historical Institute (CHI) for the historic photos and tireless archival support; and to Peter Reske for his invaluable assistance in reading through this manuscript prior to publication.*

In May 1911, the English Evangelical Lutheran Synod of Missouri and Other States (English Synod) met in convention for the last time at Redeemer Lutheran Church, St. Louis. Simultaneously, the Deutsche Evangelisch-Lutherische Synode von Missouri, Ohio und anderen Staaten (German Missouri Synod) met in convention just a mile away at Holy Cross Lutheran Church, St. Louis. After twenty-three years of "separate, but equal," the English Synod was about to become the English District of the Missouri Synod.

The union of these two synods was at the forefront of discussion for both conventions, and both bodies eventually approved the agreed-upon terms of union at their respective conventions. On Monday, May 15, at the close of the final English Synod Convention, the delegates solemnly marched *en masse* from Redeemer to Holy Cross where they were warmly greeted by German Missouri. Adolph H. A. Biewend (1845–1919) of German Missouri delivered a speech in English, to which President Henry P. Eckhardt (1866–1949) of the English District responded. Frederick G. Kuegele (1846–1916), the first president of the English Synod, then delivered a speech in German, to which newly elected President J. Friedrich Pfotenhauer (1859–1939) of the German Synod responded. The ceremony concluded with the singing of Luther's German Te Deum and praying together the Lord's Prayer.[1]

---

[1] [George] L.[uecke], "The Convention of Synod," *Lutheran Witness* 30, no. 11 (1911): 84–85.

The Proceedings of the English Synod record the import of this event:

> The words spoken on that occasion will never be forgotten by those who were fortunate to be present on that memorable afternoon. The Spirit of God moved us deeply. We all felt the importance of what was transpiring.[2]

A year later, the union of the English Synod with German Missouri was blessed with the birth of a new, English-language hymnal—the *Evangelical Lutheran Hymn-Book* (*ELHB* 1912). This new hymnal, with tunes, was a completely revised and expanded edition of the *Evangelical Lutheran Hymn Book* (*ELHB* 1889), which had been presented and adopted nearly a quarter century earlier at the very first convention of the English Synod. As such, *ELHB* 1912 became the first English-language hymnal of the Missouri Synod and clearly pointed this predominantly German-speaking church body toward its future in worship and song in an English-speaking America.

This study will explore the formation histories of these two English Synod hymnals: *ELHB* 1889, and its revision in *ELHB* 1892; and *ELHB* 1912 and the twenty-year journey toward its publication. Toward that end, we will examine the source hymnals used by August Crull as editor and compiler of *ELHB* 1889 in selecting its core German hymns. We will then examine the non-Missouri hymnals Crull used as sources for selecting the English-language hymns of *ELHB* 1889. Proceeding chronologically, we will then explore the formation of these English Synod hymnals—from the intricacies of Crull's initial involvement in compiling *ELHB* 1889, to the long journey of the English Synod and its publication of *ELHB* 1912. This study will demonstrate that the editors of these hymnals drew almost exclusively from the German hymnal of the Missouri Synod for their German-language hymn texts as well as thematic organization of the hymns; and that they drew heavily from the hymnals of the older American Lutheran church bodies for their selection of English-language hymn texts in use by American Evangelicals of the day.

---

[2] "Proceedings of the Twelfth Convention of the Evangelical Lutheran Synod of Missouri and Other States," in St. Louis, 1911 (St. Louis: Concordia Publishing House), 73.

C. F. W. Walther and KELG 1847

When C. F. W. Walther (1811–87) and the Saxons arrived in Missouri in 1838–39, they brought with them the German-language hymnal they had used in their homeland. That hymnal was the *Dresdnisches Gesangbuch,* first published in 1796 under the oversight of Church Superintendent Karl Christian Tittmann (1744–1820).³ Concerning this hymnal, hymnologist Christoph Albrecht notes:

Figure 1: Young C. F. W. Walther, circa 1840.

In Dresden there appeared in 1796 a typical Enlightenment hymnal. In the national newspaper, there was an article that demonstrates the overconfidence typical of this period. It noted: "We should have no need of a new hymnal for centuries because Dr. Tittmann has provided the Dresden Hymnal with the greatest possible perfection, and the proper doctrine, as is here submitted in the selected songs, is exalted above all other improvements." Ironically, the Enlightenment's hymnals were among the shortest-lived in hymn-book history.⁴

---

³   The second edition was printed in 1798. See *Dresdnisches Gesangbuch auf höchsten Befehl herausgegeben,* (Dresden: Churfürstl. Hofbuchdruckerey, 1798). See also Paul Tschackert, "Tittmann, Karl Christian," in *Allgemeine Deutsche Biographie* (1894), 38: 387–88.

⁴   Christoph Albrecht, *Einführung in die Hymnologie* (Göttingen: Vandenhoeck und Ruprecht, 1973), 95: "In Dresden erschien in Jahre 1796 ein typisches Aufklärungsgesangbuch. In der Nationalzeitung war darüber ein Aufsatz zu lesen, der von der Selbsteingenommenheit dieser Epoche in bezeichnender Weise Aufschluß gibt. Es heißt darin: 'Bei uns kann das Bedürfnis eines neuen Gesangbuchs in Jahrhunderten nicht eintreten, denn es hat Dr. Tittmann dem Dresdnischen Gesangbuch die möglichste Vollkommenheit gegeben, und die rechte Lehre, wie sie hier in auserwählten Liedern vorgetragen wird, ist über alle Verbesserung erhaben.' Ausgerechnet die Aufklärungsgesangbücher gehörten aber zu den kurzlebigsten in der Gesangbuchgeschichte."

Tittmann's hymnal, produced under the influence of German Rationalism, continued to be reprinted as late as 1837, just a year before Walther and the Saxons immigrated to Missouri.[5] This was therefore the hymnal that Walther and his young colleagues grew up with, that they and their compatriots brought with them to America, and which was consequently in use at Trinity Congregation, St. Louis, when Walther began service there as pastor in May 1841.[6]

The minutes of Trinity Congregation indicate that for most of 1842, the congregation's attention was consumed with the details of constructing a new sanctuary. Shortly after the dedication of the sanctuary, however, the congregation resolved in February 1843 that in the public divine services, only pure Lutheran hymns should be used.[7] Finally, in November 1845, the congregation resolved to publish a new hymnal toward that end.[8]

Nineteenth months later, the *Kirchengesangbuch für Evangelisch-Lutherische Gemeinden ungeänderter Augsburgischer Confession* (*KELG* 1847) was printed in New York City under the auspices of Trinity Congregation, St. Louis and shipped to St. Louis for distribu-

---

[5] *Dresdner Gesangbuch auf höchsten Befehl herausgegeben*, (Dresden and Leipzig: B. G. Teubner, 1837).

[6] In a sermon dated Advent 1842, Walther makes the following reference to the Dresden Hymnal as being in common use at Trinity Congregation: "Lasset uns zuvor Gott im stillen Gebete um seinen Gnadenbeistand anrufen, wenn wir mit einander werden gesungen haben (Dresdner Gesangb.) 225, 9." ["Let us before God in silent prayer call upon his gracious assistance, as soon as we have sung with one another (Dresden Hymnal) 225:9."]. C. F. W. Walther, *Gnadenjahr: Predigten über die Evangelien des Kirchenjahrs von Dr. C. F. W. Walther. Aus seinem schriftlichen Nachlaß gesammelt* (St. Louis: Concordia Publishing House, 1891), 31. Walther could not have so specifically referenced a hymn number and stanza, had not that hymnal been readily available to the worshipper. The parenthetical reference appears to be an editorial insertion made decades later, so as to not be confused with *KELG* 1847.

[7] "Minutes of Trinity Congregation, St. Louis, Missouri," CHI, St. Louis, Missouri, February 3, 1843: "In dem öffentlichen Gottesdienste dürften nur reinlutherische Lieder und bei allen Amtshandlungen nur reinlutherische Formuläen gebraucht werden."

[8] Ibid., November 17, 1845.

tion.⁹ It contained 437 hymns, as well as a selection of prayers, the Small Catechism, the Augsburg Confession, and other materials. In the 1857 printing, an appendix with six additional hymns was included; the 1917 edition added a second appendix with an additional 41 hymns.¹⁰

When one examines the Dresden hymnal that Walther and the Saxons brought with them and that was in use at Trinity Congregation, St. Louis prior to 1847, one finds little correspondence with respect to the outline and organization of the hymns found in *KELG* 1847. However, when one examines the older generation of Dresden hymnals—specifically, those published before 1796¹¹— the outline and organization of the hymns resemble very much

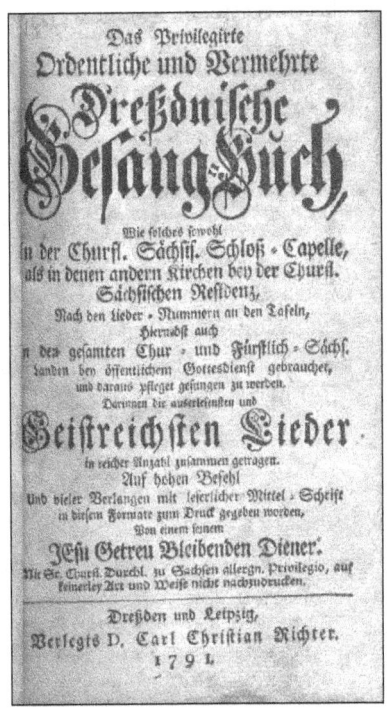

Figure 2: Title page of the 1791 Dresden Hymnal on which Walther modeled KELG 1847.

---

9   Jon D. Vieker, "The Doctrine of Baptism as Confessed by C. F. W. Walther's *Gesangbuch* of 1847" (STM Thesis, Concordia Seminary, St. Louis, 1990), 17. Much of *KELG* 1847 has recently been made available in English as Matthew Carver, trans., *Walther's Hymnal: Church Hymnbook for Evangelical Lutheran Congregations of the Unaltered Augsburg Confession* (St. Louis: Concordia Publishing House, 2012).

10 For more on the *KELG* 1917 revision project, see the series of reports in *Lehre und Wehre:* "Unser Kirchengesangbuch: I. Revision der Angaben unter den Liedern," *Lehre und Wehre* 54 (1908): 355–63; "Unser Kirchengesangbuch: II. Verzeichnis der Liederdichter," *Lehre und Wehre* 54 (1908): 448–56; "Unser Kirchengesangbuch: III. Die Melodienagaben," *Lehre und Wehre* 55 (1909): 198–204; and "Unser Kirchengesangbuch: IV. Vermehrung des Liederbestandes," *Lehre und Wehre* 55 (1909): 481–98.

11 For example, *Das Privilegirte Ordentliche und Vermehrte Dresdnische Gesang-Buch*, (Dresden and Leipzig: Verlegts D. Carl Christian Richter,

the outline that Walther adopted for the hymnal of 1847.[12] Walther's preference for the confessional Lutheran theology he found in such "old" German hymnals is further evidenced in an 1850 article in *Der Lutheraner*, where the writer notes:

> ... only the *old* hymn books—which are also now and then in this land found among immigrant German Lutherans, such as the *old* Dresden, the *old* Marburg, the *old* Silesian, the Pomeranian, Prussian, Hamburger, Bayreuther, etc.—exhibit a sufficiently large stock of the *old* pure Lord's Supper hymns containing the teachings of the Lutheran Church. And whoever has no such *old* hymnal in his possession, this alone should be enough to convince him to get the "St. Louis Lutheran Hymnal."[13]

For Walther, *KELG* 1847 represented a repudiation of the Rationalist hymnals of his day and a restoration of the "old," pre-1796, Dresden line of hymnals, fine-tuned to engage German Lutherans in America as the first hymnal of the Missouri Synod.[14]

Walther's *KELG* became the first and only German hymnal the

1791).

[12] Vieker, "Walther's Gesangbuch of 1847," 29–38.

[13] "Die Gesang-Bücher," *Der Lutheraner* 7 (1850): 35: "... allein, die alten Gesangbücher, die auch noch hin und wieder hier zu Lande bei eingewanderten deutschen Lutheranern zu finden sind, als das alte Dresdner, das alte Marburger, das alte Schlesinger, das Pommersche, Preußische, Hamburger, Baireuther u. zeigen zur Genüge, daß ein großer Vorrath alter reiner Abendmahlslieder, welche die Lehre der Lutherischen Kirche enthalten, vorhanden sind; und wer etwa kein solches altes Gesangbuch im Besitz hätte, der könnte sich aus dem 'Lutherischen St. Louis Gesangbuch' genug davon überzeugen." Emphasis not original. As editor-in-chief of *Der Lutheraner*, it is likely that Walther penned this article.

[14] Walther's pattern of "reaching back" beyond the Rationalist worship materials of his day to older, orthodox resources has also been observed in his editing of the baptismal order for his *Kirchen-Agende für evangelisch-lutherische Gemeinden ungeänderter Augsburgischer Confession*, (St. Louis: Druckerei der Deutschen Ev.-Luth. Synode v. Missouri, O. u. a. St., 1856). See Norman Nagel, "Holy Baptism and Pastor Walther," in *Light for Our World: Essays Commemorating the 150th Anniversary of Concordia Seminary, St. Louis, Missouri*, ed. John W. Klotz (St. Louis: Concordia Seminary, 1989), 61–82.

Missouri Synod would ever have, available for purchase from Concordia Publishing House even into the 1960s.[15] Edited by the synod's founding president and foremost theologian, *KELG* became for Missouri Lutherans a kind of hymnological icon and theological plumb line against which all subsequent hymnals would be measured.

KELG 1847 and Transitional English-Language Hymnals

Over three decades later, the Lutheran Publishing House in Decorah, Iowa published the *Hymn Book for the Use of Evangelical Lutheran Schools and Congregations*, a modest collection of 130 hymns in English.[16] Also called the "Decorah Hymnal," this slender volume contained the translations and compilations of the young August Crull (1845–1923), who would later become the editor and compiler of *ELHB* 1889. Shortly after the publication of DH 1879, Walther wrote a glowing review in *Der Lutheraner*, in which he declared:

> It is with great pleasure that we hasten to report to our readers the publication of a booklet with the above title. It is a pure, admittedly small, but complete, English-Lutheran school and church hymnal. . . . We call it a *pure* hymnal because it contains only those English hymns that not only contain no false doctrine, but also breathe a truly evangelical spirit. More than half of them (72), so far as we are able to judge, are in form and content admirably successful English translations of the best hymns of our German Evangelical-Lutheran Church.

---

[15] James L. Brauer, "The Hymnals of The Lutheran Church—Missouri Synod" (STM Thesis, Concordia Seminary, 1967), 42, noted in 1967 that ". . . the *Kirchengesangbuch für Evangelisch-Lutherische Gemeinden* may still be purchased from Concordia Publishing House. . . ." For more on the formation of *KELG* 1847, see Jon D. Vieker, "C. F. W. Walther: Editor of Missouri's First and Only German Hymnal," *Concordia Historical Institute Quarterly* 65 (1992): 53–69.

[16] *Hymn Book for the Use of Evangelical Lutheran Schools and Congregations*, (Decorah, IA: Lutheran Publishing House, 1879). This collection was published by the Norwegian Evangelical Lutheran Church in America, at that time in fellowship with the Missouri Synod through the Synodical Conference.

Walther argues that the Decorah Hymnal is doctrinally pure because even though it is in English and includes hymns that were written by non-Lutherans, there is no false doctrine to be found among them. On the contrary, these hymns breathe a "truly evangelical spirit," the great majority of them successful English translations of the best hymns from German Lutheranism.[17] In other words, like the hymns of *KELG* 1847, these hymns proclaim the pure Gospel. Walther continues:

We call the book a *complete* hymnal, however, not because it is a comprehensive, English, let alone German-Lutheran, hymn treasury, but rather because it contains the requisite number of selections for the most relevant situations. Of course over time, the increasingly large flood of the number of hymns in our church hymnals has become more of a hindrance than a furtherance of the blessings that come with hymns. Originally, almost every Lutheran Christian could sing from memory all the hymns in use at church, and thus carried with him, by and by, an exceedingly rich, spiritual treasure. Even Caspar Neumann writes in his Silesian hymnal of 1737: "My people would be ashamed if they had to look down at their hymnals to sing." When one is in the habit of looking to certain hymns for a particular doctrine or occasion, and then finding in not only

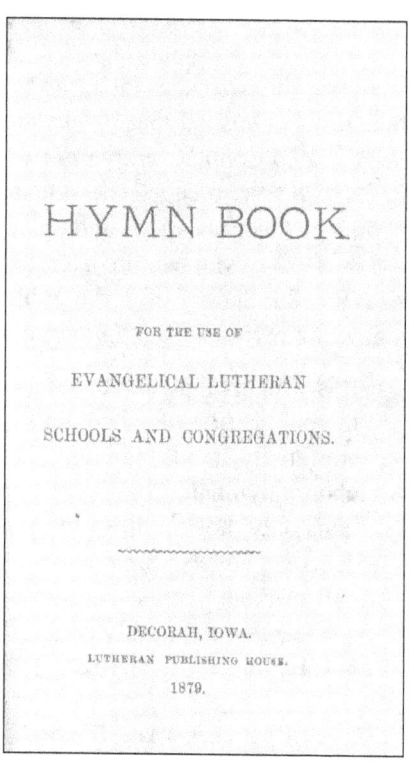

Figure 3: Title page of DH 1879.

---

[17] In fact, 81 hymn texts in the Decorah Hymnal appear to come from the German, 11 from either Latin, Danish, or Norwegian, and 38 originally composed in English.

a great many otherwise good hymnals certain, so to speak, made-to-order songs of little poetic value, it happens also that due to the sheer quantity of hymns as well as the resulting massive change [involved in using them], that the familiarity of Christians with their very best hymns becomes less and less.[18]

Walther suggests that bigger and newer are not necessarily better. He laments the many "made-to-order songs of little poetic value" which are found even in "a great many otherwise good hymnals." The un-

---

[18] C. F. W. Walther, "Review of *Hymn Book for the Use of Evangelical Lutheran Schools and Congregations*," *Der Lutheraner* 35 (1879): 104: "Mit großer Freude beeilen wir uns, unseren Lesern das Erschienen eines Büchleins mit vorstehendem Titel zu melden. Es ist dasselbe ein reines, zwar kleines, aber vollständiges englisch-lutherisches Schul- und Kirchengesangbuch. . . . Wir nennen es ein reines Gesangbuch, weil sich darin nur solche englische Kirchenlieder befinden, welche nichts nur keine falsche Lehre enthalten, sondern auch einen wahrhaft evangelischen Geist athmen. Mehr als die Hälfte derselben (72) sind, so weit wir dies zu beurtheilen vermögen, nach Form und Inhalt vortrefflich gelungene englisch Uebersetzungen der besten deutschem Lieder unserer ev.-lutherischen Kirche. Ein vollständiges Gesangbuch nennen wir das Büchlein allerdings nicht darum, weil dasselbe den ganzen englisch-, geschweige deutsch-lutherischen Liederschatz, sondern weil es für alle betreffenden Fälle die nöthige Auswahl enthält. Ist doch die im Laufe der Zeit immer größer gewordenen Anschwellung der Zahl der Lieder in unseren Kirchengesangbüchern eher eine Hinderung, als eine Förderung des Liedersegens geworden. Fast jeder lutherische Christ konnte anfänglich alle in der Kirche im Gebrauch befindlichen Lieder auswendig und trug damit einen überaus köstlichen geistlichen Schatz fort und fort bei sich. Noch Caspar Neumann schreibt in seinem schlesischen Gesangbuch von Jahre 1737: 'Meine Leute würden sich schämen, wenn sie unter dem Singen in das Buch sehen sollten.' Nachdem man darauf bedacht gewesen ist, für jede Lehre und Gelegenheit eigene Lieder zu suchen, finden sich nicht nur selbst in sonst guten Gesangbüchern gar manche, so zu sagen, auf Bestellung gemachte Lieder namentlich von wenig poetischem Werte, es ist auch durch die Menge und den durch dieselbe veranlaßten großen Wechsel die Bekanntschaft der Christen mit ihren besten Kirchenliedern eine immer geringere geworden." Emphasis original. Walther's review was later translated into Norwegian and adapted for the Norwegian Church's periodical, *Evangelisk Luthersk Kirketidende* 6, no. 37 (September 12, 1879): 591–92.

Figure 4: Title page of Lutheran Hymns *(1882).*

fortunate result has been an "increasingly large flood" of hymn texts, which, Walther suggests, has actually hindered the blessings of knowing hymns by heart as well as where to look in the hymnal for a hymn with a particular doctrinal emphasis or occasion. As a result, the small but select number of core hymns in DH 1879 could actually be considered a virtue, in Walther's estimation.

Two even smaller English-language hymn collections appeared during the decade following. In 1882, *Lutheran Hymns. For the Use of English Lutheran Missions,* a collection of 18 German hymn translations by Martin Guenther (1831–93) and Carl Janzow (1847–1911), was published by Concordia Publishing House.[19] Concerning this collection, Guenther, who was also editor of *Der Lutheraner* at the time, commented:

> The English-language missionary does not everywhere find orthodox English hymnals. In order that he can now have orthodox hymns sung in his church services, it has seemed necessary to have a number of them printed. The above collection contains 16 [18] hymns and some verses . . . [Here follow the titles of 13 of the hymns.] . . . The English is connected *as closely as possible* to the German text. The hymns are included with 15 melodies. Perhaps many German congregations will also be served by this collection, which, if they occasionally

---

[19] *Lutheran Hymns. For the Use of English Lutheran Missions*, (St. Louis: Concordia Publishing House, 1882). See also Carl F. Schalk, *God's Song in a New Land: Lutheran Hymnals in America* (St. Louis: Concordia Publishing House, 1995), 151.

hold English services (for example, for church dedications, New Year's festivals, etc.) sometimes find themselves in a bit of a dilemma when it comes to their hymns.[20]

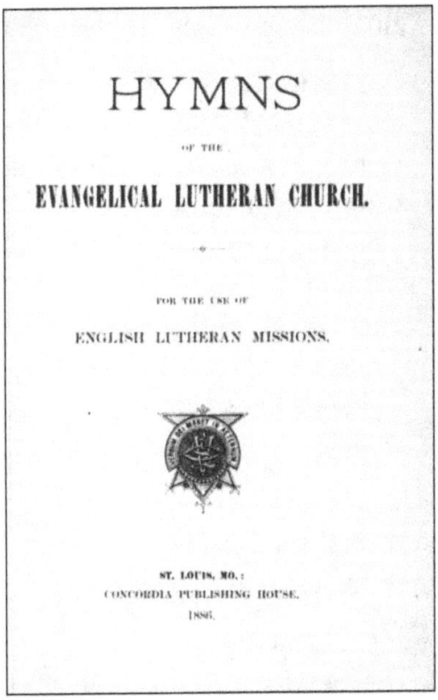
HYMNS

OF THE

EVANGELICAL LUTHERAN CHURCH.

FOR THE USE OF

ENGLISH LUTHERAN MISSIONS.

ST. LOUIS, MO.:

CONCORDIA PUBLISHING HOUSE.

1886.

Figure 5: Title page of Hymns of the Evangelical Lutheran Church *(1886).*

Guenther's comments reflect some of the challenges facing German Missouri's pastors and congregations in reaching out to an English-speaking America in the 1880s. Like Walther, Guenther's concern was to find orthodox, Lutheran hymns for use in English, and that happened best, in his estimation, by translating the core German hymns of the Lutheran Church into good, idiomatic English.

A second, more substantial collection appeared just four years later under the editorship of August Crull. With a title very similar to the Guenther collection, *Hymns of the Evangelical Lutheran Church. For the Use of English Lutheran Missions,* Crull's collection contained 33 hymns with their melodies.[21] Only a year before his death,

20 Martin Guenther, "Review of *Lutheran Hymns. For the Use of English Lutheran Missions,*" *Der Lutheraner* 38 (1882): 56: "Unser englischer Missionar findet nicht überall rechtgläubige englische Gesangbücher. Damit er nun rechtgläubige Lieder in den Gottesdiensten singen lassen könne, hat man für nötig erachtet, eine Anzahl drucken zu lassen. Die obigen Sammlung enthält 16 Lieder und einige Verse; darunter . . . Dies Englisch schließt sich *so genau als möglich* an den deutschen Text an. Den Liedern sind 15 Melodien beigegeben. Vielleicht ist mit dieser Sammlung auch mancher deutschen Gemeinde gedient, die, wenn sie gelegentlich z. B. bei Kirchweihen, Neujahrsfesten u., einen englischen Gottesdienst halten, wegen der Lieder in Verlegenheit kommen." Emphasis original.

21 August Crull, ed. *Hymns of the Evangelical Lutheran Church. For the Use of English Lutheran Missions* (St. Louis: Concordia Publishing House, 1886).

Walther reviewed this collection in *Der Lutheraner* and noted:

> A review copy of this new collection of Lutheran hymns in the English language has just now come into our hands. We are happy to make our readers acquainted with the appearance of this volume. The selection of songs seems to us to be quite excellent. The book actually contains the core of Lutheran hymns in English translation, and as far as we can judge, faithfully provides translations of the German originals into idiomatic English. There are 33 songs appearing under six headings [*Rubriken*]....[22]

As with *KELG* 1847 and its Dresden predecessors, the outline and arrangement of hymns was an important consideration for Walther, and he lists the six general headings or "rubrics" [*Rubriken*] under which the various hymns were placed:

1. General Hymns for the Divine Service [*Allgemeine Gottesdienst-Lieder*].
2. Church Year [*Kirchenjahr*]
3. Means of Grace [*Gnadenmittel*]
4. Order of Salvation [*Heilsordnung*]
5. Christian Life [*Christliche Leben*]
6. Death and Eternity [*Tod und Ewigkeit*]

Appendix One lists an aggregate compilation of the German-language hymns found in the three English-language hymn collections that appeared during the decade prior to *ELHB* 1889. It also shows where those hymns first appeared in *KELG* 1847 and then which of them were subsequently included in *ELHB* 1889.

Of the 80 German-language hymns listed in Appendix One, there

---

[22] C. F. W. Walther, "Review of *Hymns of the Evangelical Lutheran Church*," *Der Lutheraner* 42, no. 7 (1886): 56: "Soeben kommt diese neue Sammlung lutherischer Kirchenlieder in englischer Sprache zum Zweck einer Anzeige derselben in unsere Hände. Mit Freuden machen wir unsere Leser mit dem Erscheinen derselben hierdurch bekannt. Die getroffene Auswahl der Lieder scheint uns eine ganz vortreffliche zu sein. Das Büchlein enthält wirklich den Kern der Lutherischen Kirchenlieder in englischer Uebersetzung, und soweit wir es beurtheilen können, gibt die Uebersetzung die deutschen Originale ebenso treu, als in echtem Englisch wieder. Die Zahl der Lieder ist 33. Sie ist unter sechs Rubriken gebracht."

were only five that never appeared in *KELG* 1847. From the other side, there were only five hymns of the 80 that never made it into *ELHB* 1889 from the predecessor volumes, and four of those were the same hymns that never appeared in *KELG* 1847.[23]

Appendix One suggests several important considerations. First of all, it provides a corpus of *Kernlieder* from German Missouri's perspective. In other words, these could be considered the core, German hymn texts, distilled from *KELG* 1847, that were viewed as most critical to be transmitted into English. Secondly, other than the few exceptions mentioned above, virtually all of the German hymns found in English translation in the three predecessor hymn collections were eventually included in *ELHB* 1889. Thus, these three predecessor collections appear to have served as a means for vetting various translations during the decade prior to *ELHB* 1889. Above all, Appendix One demonstrates the profound dependence of *ELHB* 1889 on *KELG* as the primary source for its German hymnody.

ELHB *1889 and Hymnals from Other Lutheran Churches*

As *KELG* became the primary source for the German-language hymnody that was brought into *ELHB* 1889, so also were the hymnals of the older, Lutheran church bodies in America the primary sources for the English-language hymnody that was included in *ELHB* 1889. Yet, this marriage of old and new, German and English hymnody, did not come about without some tensions for Missouri Synod Lutherans.

For instance, in 1883, Walther was asked his opinion as to "whether it is advisable to introduce the singing of Methodist songs in a Lutheran Sunday School."[24] Walther's response was, in short, "No, this

---

[23] Two of these hymns were eventually included in a later edition of *ELHB*: "Lord, to Thee I Make Confession" (*ELHB* 1912, no. 416) and "Tender Shepherd, Thou Hast Stilled" (*ELHB* 1912, no. 537).

[24] C. F. W. Walther, "Letter to L. H. Lorentz, January 23, 1883," Wadewitz Transcriptions, CHI, St. Louis, Missouri. English translation in C. F. W. Walther, "Methodist Hymns in a Lutheran Sunday School: Theological Opinion by C. F. W. Walther," in *At Home in the House of My Fathers: Presidential Sermons, Essays, Letters, and Addresses from the Missouri Synod's Great Era of Unity and Growth*, ed. Matthew C. Harrison (St.

is not advisable, rather very incorrect and pernicious." Walther then went on to offer six reasons for his decidedly negative response, summarized as follows:

1. Because our church already has such a rich hymnody, introducing Methodist hymns would be like "carrying coals to Newcastle." Thirty or forty years ago this might have been understandable, with the scarcity of songbooks for Lutheran children, but today the church has everything it needs in this regard.

2. Preachers have the holy duty to provide only "pure spiritual food" to those entrusted to their care, and it would be "soul-murder" [*Seelenmord*] to set before children such poisonous food. Even if the preacher claims that he is allowing only "correct" hymns, there is no excuse since:
   a) the true Lutheran spirit is found in none of them;
   b) our Lutheran hymns are more powerful, substantive, and sober-minded [*nüchterner*];
   c) any Methodist hymns dealing with the sacraments are completely in error; and
   d) these hymnals will cause our little ones to read and sing also the noticeably false hymns that are found in them.

3. Any preacher who openly introduces Methodist hymns, let alone hymnals, raises the suspicion that he is "no true Lutheran at heart," but rather a "unionistic man" . . . "a mingler of religions and churches" [*ein Religionsmenger und Kirchenmischer*].

4. As a result, such practice also leads our children to hold a similar "unionistic sentiment," to grow up and eventually leave the Lutheran Church and join the Methodists.

5. By purchasing Methodist hymnals, one is subsidizing "Methodist fanatics in their horrible errors," such that the Methodists will even come to believe that we Lutherans must think Methodism to be better than Lutheranism.

6. The entire Lutheran congregation is given offense and

Louis: Concordia Publishing House, 2011), 331–32.

even led to believe that Methodists have a better faith than Lutherans.

Walther's argument revolves around three basic elements. The first is an appeal to the already rich treasury of "powerful, substantive, and sober-minded" Lutheran hymns, and that it therefore would make no sense to introduce Methodist hymns into a Lutheran congregation. A second element is doctrinal and pastoral—that Methodist hymns would purvey false doctrine into a Lutheran congregation, like feeding a spiritual poison to little children. Without any appeal to the specific, Walther asserts that the "true Lutheran spirit" is found in none of these hymns, and that were any to deal with the sacraments, they would certainly be completely in error.

A third element of Walther's argument, however, appears to reflect a Missouri Synod constitutional concern with introducing a heterodox, Methodist hymnal into a Lutheran congregation. Walther suggests that to do so would not only subsidize Methodists and thereby affirm them in their error, but it would also give the impression that such a pastor is unionistic, "a mingler of religions and churches" [*Religionsmenger und Kirchenmischer*].[25] Walther's vocabulary here is reminiscent of the conditions for membership outlined in the Missouri Synod's constitution of 1847, which required "separation from all commixture of Church or faith [*Kirchen- und Glaubensmengerei*], as, for example, serving of mixed congregations by a servant of the Church; taking part in the service and Sacraments of heretical or mixed congregations; taking part in any tract distribution and mission projects, etc."[26] The constitution continues with a further condition for membership:

---

[25] Walther, "Letter to L. H. Lorentz, January 23, 1883": ". . . daß er also ein Unionsmann, ein Religionsmenger und Kirchenmischer ist."

[26] *Die Verfassung der deutschen evangelisch- lutherischen Synode von Missouri, Ohio und anderen Staaten*, (St. Louis: Weber & Olshausen, 1846), 5: "Lossagung von aller Kirchen- und Glaubensmengerei, als da ist: Das Bedienen gemischter Gemeinden, als solcher, von Seiten der Diener der Kirche; Theilnahme an dem Gottesdienst und den Sacramentshandlungen falschgläubiger und gemischter Gemeinden, Theilnahme an allem falschgläubigen Traktaten- und Missionswesen, u.s.w." English translation from Gustave Polack, "Our First Synodical Constitution," *Concordia Historical Institute Quarterly* 16, no. 1 (1943): 3.

The exclusive use of doctrinally pure church books and schoolbooks. (Agenda, hymnals, readers, etc.) If it is impossible in some congregations to replace immediately the unorthodox hymnals and the like with orthodox ones, then the pastor of such a congregation can become a member of Synod only if he promises to use the unorthodox hymnal only under open protest and to strive in all seriousness for the introduction of an orthodox hymnal.[27]

Thus, the force of Walther's argument is focused against the introduction of a Methodist *hymnal* into a Lutheran congregation. His argument does not directly engage the question as to whether it would be appropriate to sing *hymns* written by Methodists or whether some hymns used by Methodists might also be theologically appropriate for Lutherans to use. For Walther, the central issue revolved around the use of a Methodist *hymnal* in a Missouri Synod congregation. Introducing a Methodist hymnal into a Missouri Synod congregation constituted a violation of the conditions of membership in the synod. Since it was self-evident that a Methodist hymnal would contain false doctrine (especially with regard to the sacraments), that fact alone disqualified it for use in Missouri Synod congregations, which all agree to the "exclusive use of doctrinally pure church books and schoolbooks. (Agenda, hymnals, readers, etc.)." Walther further suggests that in using a Methodist hymnal, Lutheran children and congregation members would surely read and sing some of the hymns that contain false doctrine. In doing so, they were at risk of becoming indifferent to the theological differences between Lutherans and Methodists, with the result that they may even someday leave the Lutheran Church and join the Methodist Church instead.

Although Walther was opposed in principle to the use of Methodist hymnals in a Lutheran congregation, he was not beyond examining the specifics and giving his blessing to a Lutheran hymnal that contained hymns written by Methodists and other Protestants. Just a few years earlier, Walther had described DH 1879 as "a *pure* hymnal because it contains only those English hymns that not only contain

---

[27] *Die Verfassung der deutschen evangelisch- lutherischen Synode von Missouri, Ohio und anderen Staaten*, 5. English translation from, Polack, "Our First Synodical Constitution," 3.

(1 Decorah H. B. 2-Church Book. 3-Book of Worship.
4-Ohio Hymnal.)

INDEX OF FIRST LINES. *

		NO.
2 4 **A** great and mighty wonder — *Anatolius.—J. M. Neale, Tr.*		16
2 4 A hymn of glory let us sing - *Beda—E. R. Charles, Tr.*		99
—— A Lamb goes uncomplaing forth - - *Composite.*		58
—— A mighty Fortress is our God - *Church Book, Tr. a.*		135
—— Abide, O dearest Jesus - - - - *A. Crull, Tr,*		2
1 2 3 4 Abide with me ! fast falls the eventide - *H. F. Lyte.*		368
—— Again is come the new church-year - - *Comp.*		15
—— Ah God, my days are dark indeed - - - *Comp.*		335
—— Ah Lord our God, let them not be confounded - - *C. Winkworth, Tr. a*		336
1 2 3 4 Alas ! and did my Saviour bleed - - - *I. Watts.*		59
—— Alas, my God ! my sins are great *C. Winkworth, Tr. a*		187
—— All glory be to God on high - *C. Winkworth, Tr. a*		1
2 3 All hail the power of Jesus' name - - - *From E. Perronet, a*		222
—— All my heart this night rejoices - - - *Comp.*		17
—— All praise to Jesus' hallowed name - *R. Massie, Tr. a*		18
2 3 All that I was, my sin, my guilt - - *H. Bonar, ?*		204
—— All things hang on our possessing - - - *C. Winkworth, Tr. a*		243
1 2 3 4 Almighty God, Thy Word is cast - *From J. Cawood*		3
2 3 4 Am I a soldier of the Cross - - ; *I. Watts, a*		244
2 3 And let this feeble body fail - - - *C. Wesley, a*		337
2 3 4 And must this body die - - - - *I. Watts, a*		369
3 4 And will the Judge descend - - - - *P. Doddridge*		387
2 4 And wilt Thou pardon, Lord - - - *Jos.-of the Studium-J. M. Neale, Tr.*		188
3 4 Angels from the realms of glory - - *A. Steele.*		53
2 3 Approach, my soul, the mercy seat - - *J. Newton.*		205
2 3 Arise, my soul, arise - - - - *C. Wesley. a.*		206
—— Arise, sons of the Kingdom - - - - *Comp,*		19
1 2 3 4 Asleep in Jesus ! blessed sleep - - - *M. Mackay.*		370
2 4 As with gladness men of old - - - *W. C. Dix*		50
—— Awake, my heart, with gladness - *J. Kelly, Tr. a.*		88
1 2 3 4 Awake, my soul, and with the sun - *Th. Ken, a.*		286
3 4 Awake, my soul, in joyful lays - - *S. Medley, a.*		310

Figure 6: *Excerpt from "Index of First Lines" from* ELHB *1889.*

no false doctrine, but also breathe a truly evangelical spirit."[28] Thus, when August Crull began compiling the hymns for *ELHB* 1889, his previous work in compiling DH 1879 a decade earlier utilizing Walther's hermeneutic (selecting only those hymns that "contain no false doctrine" and "breathe a truly evangelical spirit") became foundational to his selection of English-language hymn texts. The sources Crull used to locate such hymns can be determined by an examination of the indexes included in *ELHB* 1889.

---

[28] Walther, "Review of *Hymn Book for the Use of Evangelical Lutheran Schools and Congregations*," 104.

There are two indexes included in the back of *ELHB* 1889. The second index is titled "Translations from the German" and provides the German title of the hymns that originated in German, along with an attributed author and the hymn number. This index makes it easy for someone who knows the German title of a hymn to find where in *ELHB* 1889 that hymn might be found in English. The inclusion of such an index suggests the editor's concern with demonstrating to its users that the familiar, German hymns from *KELG* 1847 were amply included in *ELHB* 1889—a concern that was carried forward by the inclusion of a similar index in every subsequent edition of *ELHB*, even through the 1931 printing of *ELHB* 1912.

The first index in *ELHB* 1889, however, is even more unique. (See Figure 6.) It is titled "Index of First Lines" and provides an alphabetical listing of the first line of every hymn as well as its hymn number. This, in itself, is not remarkable. However, this index also provides additional information, depending on whether the hymn's language of origin is German or English. For the hymns of German origin, it gives the name of the translator since the author's name is already noted in the second index. For the English-language hymns, however, it gives the name of the author of the hymn; or, if it is a translation from Latin or another language other than German, it provides the name of both the author and the translator. Most remarkable, however, is that for every hymn of non-German origin, it indicates in which of four contemporary, English-language Lutheran hymnals that hymn is found: 1) DH 1879; 2) *Church Book for the Use of Evangelical Lutheran Congregations* (*CB* 1868), the English-language hymnal of the General Council;[29] 3) *Book of Worship* (*BoW* 1870), the English-language

---

[29] Louis F. Benson, *The English Hymn: Its Development and Use in Worship* (Philadelphia: The Presbyterian Board of Publication, 1915), 560, notes that work on *CB* 1868 began in 1862 as a project of the Pennsylvania Ministerium under the guidance of Beale M. Schmucker (1827–88) and Frederick M. Bird (1838–1908). With the formation of the General Council in 1867, this collection was published a year later under the authority of the council. Of the 588 hymns in *CB* 1868, Benson notes that 167 are from the German, and 53 from either Latin or Greek. The remainder are English-language in origin, with prominence given to the hymnody of Isaac Watts and Charles Wesley. Schalk, *God's Song in a New Land*, 146, observes that "the importance of this hymnbook as representative of a specifically Lutheran hymnody . . . is somewhat mitigated by the fact that

hymnal of the General Synod;[30] and 4) the *Evangelical Lutheran Hymnal* (*ELH* 1880), the English-language hymnal of the Ohio Synod.[31] Remarkably, this first-line index does not indicate which hymns of German origin are found in these four other non-Missouri hymnals, but only those hymns that came from English.

This "Index of First Lines" in *ELHB* 1889 suggests a number of significant considerations. First, it indicates that Crull was exceedingly conscientious in providing the user with information as to which hymns were of German origin and which were from English or other languages. Thus, the first index is geared toward providing informa-

---

less than one-sixth of the total contents could in any way be described as specifically Lutheran [in origin]."

[30] Benson, *The English Hymn*, 561, notes that there were actually two Lutheran hymnals during this period with the title *Book of Worship*. After the Civil War, the General Synod of the South remained apart from the General Synod and published *Book of Worship* (Columbia, SC, 1867). The General Synod later revised its hymnal, *Hymns Selected and Original: for Public and Private Worship* (Baltimore: T. Newton Kurtz, 1852), and published the revision as *Book of Worship* (Philadelphia: Board of Publication, 1870). This latter hymnal was the source used for *ELHB* 1889. Benson, *The English Hymn*, 561, describes *BoW* 1870 as "simply a hymn book, preceded by an order of worship covering some eight pages . . . The hymns, both by omissions and additions, show growth in discrimination [from the 1852 predecessor], but none toward churchliness." Concerning the scope of hymnody in the General Synod during this period, Benson concludes: "The Hymnody itself is not Lutheran, but is drawn from outside; it may rather be described as well within the lines of the Evangelical Hymnody, though somewhat heightened in color through revivalistic influences." Benson, *The English Hymn*, 419.

[31] Schalk, *God's Song in a New Land*, 141, notes that the Ohio Synod's *ELH* 1880 represented "a vigorous return to the hymnody of the Lutheran Reformation. Of the 468 hymns it contained, 181 or almost 40 percent were translations from the German . . . Although the early English hymnody of the Ohio Synod reflected the influences of the unionism and rationalism of those days, its contacts with the Missouri Synod in the 'Free Conferences' of the 1850s and its membership in the Synodical Conference, organized in 1872, moved to strengthen and reinforce its inherent confessionalism. In its *Evangelical Lutheran Hymnal* of 1880 it went far beyond the General Council's *Church Book* of 1868 in appropriating for English-speaking Lutherans the historic heritage of Reformation hymnody."

tion as to where the English-language hymns came from (either via English translation or as English-language originals), and the second index is geared toward providing information on the hymns of German origin. Indeed, the proper balance between the core German hymnody from *KELG* 1847 and the "new" English-language hymnody from the other hymnals appears to have been a critical consideration—so much so that elsewhere in *ELHB* 1889, on a page titled "Arrangement of Hymns," Crull even tallies up the number of hymns from each heading in the hymnal to show that, according to his reckoning, a total of 203 hymns came from the German, and 197 were from the English.[32] (See Figure 7.)

The most critical factor that the first-line index in *ELHB* 1889 raises for consideration, however, is the provenance of the sources that Crull used to assemble the English-language hymnody. To summarize, the evidence suggests that Crull essentially culled through the already established English-language hymnals of non-Synodical Conference Lutherans—in particular, the General Council, the General Synod, the Ohio Synod, and the Norwegian Evangelical Lutheran Church in America. Although two of these church bodies (the Ohio Synod and the Norwegians) had been members of the Synodical Conference prior to the Predestinarian Controversy of the 1880s, it is remarkable to see the great number of hymns attributed also to the English-language hymnals of the General Council and especially the more liberal General Synod.[33]

---

[32] *ELHB* 1889, xvii.

[33] It is remarkable because this period (ca. 1880–1915) is considered by some to be one of the most polemical between the Missouri Synod and other, non-Synodical Conference Lutherans. Fred W. Meuser, "Facing the Twentieth Century," in *The Lutherans in North America*, ed. E. Clifford Nelson (Philadelphia: Fortress Press, 1980), 377–78, notes about this period: "Predestination, grace, and man's role in conversion were still the controversial issues. The decade of journalistic warfare in the 1890s, untempered by any personal contacts, had made each side . . . more confident of its position. Even more than the others, the Missouri Synod had boundless confidence that it represented the only real Lutheranism in America. . . . Friedrich Bente's editorial on the fiftieth anniversary of *Lehre und Wehre* [1904] illustrates this total confidence that Missourians had nothing to learn from Lutherans of other synods. . . . Almost every issue of *Lehre und Wehre* and *Der Lutheraner* pointed out weaknesses and

ARRANGEMENT OF HYMNS.			GERMAN.	ENGLISH.
I Sunday - - - Nos.	1– 14		6	8
II Advent and Christmas	15– 40		19	7
III New Year - - - -	41– 49		5	4
IV Epiphany - - - -	50– 52		2	1
V Presentation - - - -	53– 57		4	1
VI Passion - - - - -	58– 87		15	15
VII Easter - - - - -	88– 98		8	3
VIII Ascension - - - -	99–108		4	6
IX Pentecost - - - -	109–122		8	6
X Trinity - - - - -	123–131		5	4
XI Michaelmas - - - -	132–134		1	2
XII Reformation - - -	135–138		4	—
XIII The Word and the Church	139–170		10	22
XIV Catechism - - -	171–186		15	1
XV Repentance - - -	187–203		6	11
XVI Faith and Justification -	204–221		7	13
XVII The Redeemer - - -	222–242		9	12
XVIII The Christian Life -	243–285		19	24
XIX Morning - - - -	286–295		5	5
XX Evening - - - - -	296–309		7	7
XXI Praise - - - - -	310–334		8	17
XXII The Cross and Comfort	335–367		20	13
XXIII Death and Burial - -	368–386		12	7
XXIV Eternity - - - - -	387–400		4	10
XXV Doxologies - - - - - - -			203	197

xvii

Figure 7: "Arrangement of Hymns," where Crull tallies up the number of German and English hymns in ELHB *1889.*

Appendix Two shows how many of the English-language hymns are found in four of the four source hymnals, three of the four, two of the four, and in one of the four. It is significant to note that among the 52 hymns in the three-out-of-four-hymnal category, the greatest number of hymns are found in *CB* 1868 and then *BoW* 1870. And among the 105 hymns listed in the two out of four hymnal category, the greatest number of hymns are found in *BoW* 1870 and then *CB* 1868. Thus statistically, the role of these two non-Synodical conference hymnals is significant, indicating that Crull relied on them

---

deviations from the truth on the part of other Lutherans."

heavily as he went about filling in the 197 English-language hymns included in *ELHB* 1889.[34]

In summary, August Crull used *KELG* 1847 as the primary source for his German-language hymnody, and he used the hymnals of non-Synodical Conference Lutherans as the primary sources for his English-language hymnody in his compiling of *ELHB* 1889. And yet, the English-language hymnody was made to live within the household of the German-language hymnody—that is, all of the hymns, whether English or German in origin, were ordered within the thematic structure provided by Walther's *KELG* 1847. Appendix Three compares the arrangement of thematic headings in Walther's *KELG* 1847 with that of Crull's *ELHB* 1889. It demonstrates just how closely Crull followed Walther's thematic outline in *KELG* 1847 in the compilation of *ELHB* 1889. In fact, as one surveys the life and times of August Crull, Walther's direct interaction with and profound influence on the editor of *ELHB* 1889 become apparent.

The Life and Times of August Crull

August Crull was born in Rostock, Germany in 1845, the son of a prominent attorney.[35] Shortly after his father's untimely death, Crull's mother was remarried to Albert Friedrich Hoppe (1828–1911), a Lutheran pastor, and they immigrated to St. Louis in the fall of 1855.[36]

---

[34] Benson, *The English Hymn*, 562–63, notes: "The course of Lutheran Hymnody, as we have followed it, makes plain why that Church has done so little in the way of acclimating the old Lutheran hymns and chorals [sic] in other denominations. The English-speaking congregations wished to use the hymns of their American neighbors, and even in adopting for church use the versions of German hymns by Miss Winkworth, Mills, Massie, and others, they have been followers rather than leaders. American Lutheranism presents a curious case of an immigrant Church merging its inheritance and traditions in its new surroundings until spurred by the pressure of new immigrations to recover what it had lost."

[35] For an older and more extensive treatment of Crull's life, see: Glen Kenneth Johnson, "August Crull's Contribution to the Missouri Synod" (STM Thesis, Concordia Seminary, 1961).

[36] Ludwig Fuerbringer, "Albert Friedrich Hoppe," *Der Lutheraner* 67 (June 3, 1911): 104. In this "last will and testament," Hoppe indicates that he came to St. Louis with the personal commendation from Theodor Klief-

Figure 8: Detail of August Crull's confirmation certificate.

Crull was soon enrolled at Concordia College, a pre-seminary, preparatory school in St. Louis; and the following spring, when Crull was only eleven, his mother and step-father left him in St. Louis to serve a Missouri Synod parish in New Orleans. At age 14, Crull was confirmed at Trinity Evangelical Lutheran Church, St. Louis—where Walther was his pastor.[37]

---

oth (1810–1895)—confessional, German, "Neo Lutheran" and church Superintendent of Mecklenburg—to C. F. W. Walther. Later in life, Hoppe became the chief editor of the 23-volume "St. Louis Edition" (Walch, 2nd Edition) of Luther's writings in German.

[37] "August Crull Confirmation Certificate, April 17, 1859," August Crull Collection, CHI, St. Louis, Missouri. This document provides the most conclusive evidence of Crull's birth date (January 27, 1845), which was incorrectly noted in some of his obituaries and subsequently in some hymnals and hymnal commentaries, including: the commentary to *The Lutheran Hymnal* by W. G. Polack (1942); *Evangelical Lutheran Hymnary* (1996); the commentary to *Christian Worship: A Lutheran Hymnal* by C. T. Aufdemberge (1997); *Evangelical Lutheran Worship* (2006); and *Hymnal Companion to Evangelical Lutheran Worship* by Paul Westermeyer (2010). The certificate indicates that Crull was confirmed on April

Throughout his education, Crull excelled at his studies, particularly in languages, and he held a special fascination for all things English.[38] With a few others, he founded the first student-led group on campus, called the "Germania" society, and later also the "Polyhymnia" society.[39] He eventually enrolled in the seminary's preparatory high school in St. Louis, which was then moved to Fort Wayne during the Civil War. He returned to St. Louis in 1862 to begin his seminary training and graduated in the summer of 1865, immediately following the cessation of hostilities between North and South.[40]

Crull's first call was to Trinity Lutheran Church, Milwaukee, where he served as assistant pastor to Friedrich Lochner (1822–1911).[41] After a year, however, he resigned his call because of a chronic throat ailment and traveled to Germany to recover.[42] During his stay

---

17, 1859. It is signed by Theodor J. Brohm (1808–81), and his confirmation verse was 1 Peter 1:18–19.

[38] "Personal Notebook of August Crull," August Crull Collection, CHI, St. Louis, Missouri. This notebook contains a number of handwritten comments in German and Latin, as well as several poems in English.

[39] Otto F. Hattstaedt, "The First Literary Society in the Institutions of the Missouri Synod," *Concordia Historical Institute Quarterly* 17, no. 1 (1944): 11–14. The "Polyhymnia" society eventually became a kind of German Lutheran "glee club." Music was meticulously hand copied by each member (only the part that one needed to sing) into a notebook. For an example, see Ludwig Fuerbringer, "Music Notebook 3," 1882, Ludwig Fuerbringer Collection, CHI, St. Louis, Missouri.

[40] August Crull, "Spruch, Delivered July 4th '65," August Crull Collection, CHI, St. Louis, Missouri. This is a lengthy speech in English that Crull delivered on the July 4th after the end of the Civil War. It is full of flowery language, typical of that era, but was written with impeccable English and in Crull's meticulous handwriting. It is unclear as to where it was delivered.

[41] Friedrich Johann Carl Lochner was one of the "Sendlinge" sent by J. K. W. Löhe in the 1840s to engage in mission work in the United States. Lochner eventually became the Missouri Synod's first liturgiologist, his most significant work being *Der Hauptgottesdienst der evangelisch-lutherischen Kirche* (St. Louis: Concordia Publishing House, 1895). See also, Kevin Hildebrand, "Friedrich Lochner and *Der Hauptgottesdienst*, *Concordia Historical Institute Quarterly* 20, no. 4 (2011): 10–39.

[42] C. F. W. Walther, "To His Daughter Julie," January 8, 1866, in *Selected Letters* (St. Louis: Concordia Publishing House, 1981), 38.

in Germany, Walther wrote Crull a letter and was very concerned for his well-being. Walther urged him to return to the United States for the sake of the Missouri Synod's mission to English-speaking America. In the wake of the Civil War, Walther wrote:

> It is especially apparent to me that you, with your particular knowledge of the English language, are so capable. God has so clearly given us now a wide open door to the English public. At the same time, he is himself now preparing something great to happen—both in the South as well as in the North.
>
> How glorious it would be, therefore, if you would return home . . . It is certainly something great—yes, even the greatest thing—when God can use a poor, dying man, when he fashions such a one into his tool and intervenes, not only for the development of the history of the world, but in the history of eternity.

Figure 9: Young Pastor Crull, circa 1865, perhaps holding KELG 1847.

Walther clearly saw Crull as a key player in the Missouri Synod's future work among English-speaking America. But then he continues more specifically:

> As little as I understand of English, I have heard not only of how highly your translations of our hymns into English are touted by the experts, but I myself also realize something of their high worth, for they, with flowing beauty, so truly mirror the original.[43]

---

[43] C. F. W. Walther, "C. F. W. Walther to August Crull, March 4, 1867," in *Briefe von C. F. W. Walther an seine Freunde, Synodalgenossen und Familienglieder*, ed. Ludwig Fuerbringer, 2 vols. (St. Louis: Concordia

Clearly, Walther held Crull's work as a hymn translator in high esteem, and, if for no other reason, encouraged Crull to return to the United States.

Crull soon returned to St. Louis and worked for a few months as an editor for a local German newspaper.[44] Eventually, he was called back to Milwaukee to serve as director of a fledgling high school. Within a couple of years, however, the high school effort failed, and in 1871, Crull was called to Immanuel Lutheran Church, Grand Rapids, Michigan, where he served as the pastor of a large and fast-growing congregation.[45]

In 1873 Crull was finally called to his alma mater, Concordia College, Fort Wayne, Indiana, where he served the remainder of his career as a professor of German and French. It was from his position as college professor that Crull was able to produce a number of scholarly

---

Publishing House, 1867), 1:80–82: "Besonders wichtig ist mir, daß Sie bei Ihren sonstigen Kenntnissen der englischen Sprache so mächtig sind. Got hat nämlich offenbar uns jetzt ein weites Tor zu den englischen Publikum aufgetan. Unter demselben bereitet sich jetzt sichtlich ein großes Werk vor, ebenso in Süden wie im Norden . . . Wie herrlich wäre es daher, wenn Sie heimkehrten . . . Es ist ja etwas Großes, ja das Größte, wozu Gott einen armen Sterblichen gebrauchen kann, wenn er ihn zu einem Werkzeuge macht, das nicht nur in die Entwicklungsgeschichte der Welt, sondern in die Geschichte der Ewigkeit eingreift. . . . So wenig ich vom Englischen verstehe, so höre ich doch nicht nur, wie hoch Ihre übersetzung unserer Lieder in das Englische von Sachverständigen angeschlagen werden, ich merke auch selbst etwas von ihrem hohen Werte, da sie bei schönem Fluß das Original so treu wiedergeben." This is some of the earliest evidence of Crull translating German hymns into English. It is possible that Walther may have learned about Crull's translations during his seminary years under Walther (1862–65); or it is possible that Walther learned about them later from Crull's senior pastor, Friedrich Lochner, who was also Walther's brother-in-law.

[44] W. F. Kruse, "Professor August Crull," *Der Concordianer, Zeitschrift der Alumni Vereins des Concordia College zu Ft. Wayne, Ind.*, no. 15 (1923): 10.

[45] It was during this period that Crull likely preached the following sermon in English: August Crull, "Sermon Preached for the Dedication of the Ev. Luth. Church at Manistee, Mich., Psalm 84.1," n.d., August Crull Collection, CHI, St. Louis, Missouri. Most of the sermons in the August Crull Collection at CHI are also from this period.

and literary works in German as well as English.

In German, Crull produced two published collections of devotional poetry.[46] He also published a small pamphlet to guide high school students in proper social etiquette—a kind of "Emily Post" for German-American teens.[47] In 1893 he was commissioned by Concordia Publishing House to put into print what he had been teaching for nearly two decades—namely, a German grammar for high schoolers.[48] And shortly after Walther's death in 1887, Crull edited a monumental compilation of daily devotions in German, excerpted from the nearly half dozen volumes of Walther's published sermons.[49]

[46] The first was August Crull, *Gott tröste dich! Eine Sammlung von Trostliedern der neueren geistlichen Dichtung*, 2nd ed. (Boston: Dr. Martin Luther Waisenhaus, 1894). First published in 1889, this volume contains 240 poems by nineteenth-century German poets such as Karl Gerok (1815–90), Carl Johann Phillip Spitta (1801–59), and Julius Sturm (1816–96). Nine poems in this collection are attributed to August Crull. As the title suggests, this volume was compiled to comfort those who suffer under the cross in a variety of circumstances, and the detailed table of contents reflects that purpose.

The second volume was August Crull, *Gott segne dich!: Eine Auswahl von Stammbuchversen, Neujahrs-, Geburtstags-, Paten-, Hochzeits- und sonstigen Segenswünschen* (St. Louis: Concordia Publishing House, 1894). First printed in 1884, the poetry in this volume is also primarily from nineteenth-century German writers, but some texts from Martin Luther and Paul Gerhardt are also included. Only two poems in this collection are attributed to August Crull. In the days before "Hallmark Cards," this book provided a collection of "best wishes" that one could write to friends and loved ones for a variety of occasions—mostly in German, but also with some twelve pages in English.

[47] August Crull, *Kurze Gestenlehre: Ein Lehrbuch für hohere Schulen und zum Selbstunterricht* (St. Louis: Concordia Publishing House, 1880).

[48] August Crull, *Lehrbuch der deutschen Sprache für die unteren und mittleren Klassen höherer Schulen* (St. Louis: Concordia Publishing House, 1896). This grammar was reprinted and used by Missouri Synod institutions well into the 1920s.

[49] C. F. W. Walther, *Das Walte Gott!: Ein Handbuch zur täglichen Hausandacht aus dem Predigten des seligen C. F. W. Walther*, ed. August Crull (St. Louis: Concordia Publishing House, 1893). This volume has been recently translated into English and republished as: C. F. W. Walther, *God Grant It: Daily Devotions from C. F. W. Walther*, trans. Gerhard P. Gra-

In English, it appears that Crull was the trusted translator of Walther and, at times, of official Missouri Synod documents. For instance, as early as 1874, Crull translated a sermon by Walther on Holy Absolution, which was published in the *Lutheran Standard* and later as an offprint.[50] As the Predestinarian Controversy raged through American Lutheranism during the 1880s, Crull was Walther's chief translator of key documents and rebuttals.[51] And when the Missouri Synod prevailed in the United States Supreme Court during the early 1890s against the Bennett Law of Wisconsin and other such nativist, anti-parochial school legislation, Crull was involved in translating key synodical documents into English toward that end.[52] August Crull's greatest contribution, however, was as the editor of *ELHB* 1889.

Figure 10: Professor August Crull, circa 1900.

---

benhofer (St. Louis: Concordia Publishing House, 2006).

[50] C. F. W. Walther, *Absolution: A Sermon on John 20:19–31,* trans. August Crull (Philadelphia: Lutheran Bookstore, 1874).

[51] C. F. W. Walther, *The Controversy Concerning Predestination,* trans. August Crull (St. Louis, 1881). See also, C. F. W. Walther, *Review of Prof. Stellhorn's Tract on the Controversy Concerning Predestination,* trans. August Crull (St. Louis: Concordia Publishing House, 1881); and C. F. W. Walther, *Sermon on Predestination by C. F. W. Walther,* trans. August Crull (St. Louis: Concordia Publishing House, 1883).

[52] "Erklärung der Synode über die Schulfrage," in *Synodal-Bericht. Verhandlungen der deutschen evang.-luth. Synode von Missouri, Ohio, und anderen Staaten* (Milwaukee, Wis., 25 June–3 July 1890), 83–86.

August Crull as Editor of ELHB 1889

The genesis of the *ELHB* 1889 project is relatively obscure; no minutes or notes have survived. What has survived, however, is an intriguing series of letters[53] between August Crull and William Dallmann,[54] who at this time was serving an English Synod congregation in Baltimore. Since Dallmann was in the habit of retaining his correspondence, all of the surviving letters are from Crull, and they provide a number of helpful insights into the critical role that he played in the formation of this hymnal as well as his personal frustrations in seeing his work brought to completion by others.

In the first letter, dated May 1, 1888, Crull notes that a year earlier he had sent his initial selection of 200 "of our most familiar and best German hymns, all of them unabridged and in the meter of the original,"

---

[53] Twelve letters, in original manuscript, were examined, transcribed, and translated from German for this project. Most of the letters were written in old German handwriting, a few were in English cursive, and a couple were typewritten.

[54] Charles Frederick William Dallmann was born December 22, 1862 in Pomerania and immigrated to the United States with his family at a young age. A voracious reader in both English and German, Dallmann was encouraged by his pastor to study for the ministry and so entered Concordia College in Fort Wayne, Indiana, in 1877. From Fort Wayne, Dallmann went to Concordia, St. Louis in 1883, where he studied under C. F. W. Walther and Francis Pieper, undoubtedly attending Walther's famous "Law and Gospel" *Lutherstunden* lectures. Upon graduation in 1886, Dallmann was designated to do mission work among the English-speaking, receiving a call in 1888 to an English-language mission in Baltimore. Dallmann was editor of the *Lutheran Witness* from 1892–96, President of the English Synod from 1899–1901, an active church-planter, and most of all, a prolific author dedicated to the task of providing orthodox, Lutheran materials in the English language. See William Dallmann, *My Life: Personal Recollections of a Lutheran Missionary, Pastor, Churchman, Lecturer, Author* (St. Louis: Concordia Publishing House, 1945), 3–4, 12, 87. Dallmann's obituary in the *Lutheran Witness* noted: ". . . we owe it to William Dallmann more than to any other man that we have in The Lutheran Church—Missouri Synod an English Lutheranism that is as Scripturally sound, as confessional loyal, as pure and virile as it is today. His motto throughout his ministry was 'The faith of the fathers in the language of the children.'" Martin Walker, *Lutheran Witness* 71, no. 5 (1952): 13.

Figure 11: William Dallmann, English Synod pastor and church leader.

to the faculty at Concordia Seminary, St. Louis, "for the necessary examination."[55] It was not until several months later that Crull finally received some feedback, but then only a minimal response. A month later, Crull again writes Dallmann and indicates that he had just received word that the 200 German hymn translations have "fortunately passed and are approved by a higher place" (presumably the St. Louis faculty), and that he has subsequently sent the faculty a list of 171 English-language hymns for review. He hopes to hear back from them soon, in time to use his approaching summer vacation "for a critical establishing of the

---

[55] August Crull to William Dallmann, May 1, 1888, August Crull Collection, CHI, St. Louis, Missouri. "Leider bin ich nicht imstande, Ihnen auf Ihre Anfrage betreffs des Erscheinens des neuen engl. luth. Gesangbuches die gewünschte Antwort zu geben. Der größte und schwerste Teil der vorbereitenden Arbeit ist allerdings gethan. Zweihundert Übersetzungen unsrer bekanntesten und besten deutschen Kirchenlieder, sämtlich unverkürzt und im Versmaße des Originals, sind von mir gesammelt worden, und schon im Juli des vergangenen Jahres sandte ich dieselben der St. Louiser Fakultät behufs der nötigen Durchsicht zu. Erst nach wiederholtem Dringen erhielt ich im Anfange dieses Jahres meine Arbeit mit einigen wenigen sie begleitenden Notizen zurück. Ich ersehe daraus, daß man es mit der Publikation dieses Buches jedenfalls nicht eilig hat, und somit habe auch ich mir vorgenommen, nicht mehr die halben Nächte auf dieser Arbeit zu verwenden, damit das Buch bald- möglichst erscheinen könne, sondern die Ferienzeit zur Vollendung desselben abzuwarten. Hiernach kann das Buch jedenfalls nicht vor Neujahr 1889 im Drucke erscheinen; ob aber dann, hängt zum größten Teil von den Herren Professoren in St. Louis ab." During this period, the role of "doctrinal review" in the LCMS was performed by the seminary faculties.

text."[56] By the middle of July, however, Crull writes from his summer residence in Rome City, Indiana, and is distressed that he has not yet heard back from the St. Louis faculty. As an alternative, Crull affirms the idea (presumably offered by Dallmann) that instead of submitting the English language hymns to the St. Louis faculty, that they be submitted instead directly to the English Synod pastors for approval at their upcoming conference the following October. "They surely know the needs of the English congregations," he reasons, "much better than the gentlemen in St. Louis, or than I . . ."[57]

The October 1888 conference became the first convention of what would later be known as the "English Evangelical Lutheran Synod of Missouri and Other States," and in their newly-proposed constitution, it was noted that one of the purposes for establishing this organiza-

[56] August Crull to William Dallmann, June 11, 1888, August Crull Collection, CHI, St. Louis, Missouri. "Die 200 Übersetzungen sind glücklich absolviert und höheren Ortes approbiert. Gestern sandte ich dem Revisionscommittee in St. Louis die Titel vor 171 engl. Originalliedern zu, mit der Bitte, dieselben so bald als möglich zu prüfen, damit ich die Ferien zur kritischen Feststellung des Textes benutzen könne. Was sollte wohl sonst noch ins Gesangbuch aufgenommen werden?"

[57] August Crull to William Dallmann, July 15, 1888, August Crull Collection, CHI, St. Louis, Missouri. "Ihr freundl. Schreiben vom 9. dss ist mir von F.W. aus hierher in meine 'Sommerresidenz' nachgeschickt worden, und ich beeile mich, Ihnen mit wenigen Zeilen zu antworten. Mit dem Erscheinen des engl. Gesangbuchs hat es jedenfalls noch gute Weile, denn die Herren in St. Louis lassen sich nicht zur Eile antreiben. Vor etwa 4 Wochen sandte ich ihnen das Register der aufzunehmenden engl. Originallieder, mit der Bitte, mir ihr Urteil baldigst zuzuschicken, damit ich die Sommerferien (die einzige Zeit, die ich zu größeren Arbeiten habe) auf die Herstellung des Textes verwenden könne. Allein bis jetzt habe ich vergeblich auf Antwort gewartet. Somit werde ich wohl Ihrer Konferenz im Oktober meine Arbeit einhändigen, mit der Bitte, dieselbe zu vollenden. Denn, offen gestanden, mir vergeht die Lust, an einem Werke zu arbeiten, das beständig so gehindert wird wie dieses. Der Gedanke, das Urteil der „englischen" Pastoren einzuholen, ist übrigens sehr gut. Sie kennen das Bedürfnis der englischen Gemeinden jedenfalls viel besser als die Herren in St. L. und als ich, die wir nur nach Hörensagen urteilen können, und eine Gottesdienstordnung könnte auch wohl am besten von einer solchen Konferenz festgesetzt werden. Hinsichtlich der Originallieder stimmt Ihr Urteil vollständig mit demjenigen P. Spannaths überein, der vor einiger Zeit in dieser Angelegenheit an mich schrieb."

tion would be for "providing or recommending books, writings, papers, etc., such as liturgies, postils, *hymn-books,* catechisms, etc."[58] The hymnal, about which Crull and Dallmann had already been corresponding, was then presented to the conference, which accepted this "valuable gift" and appointed a hymnal committee consisting of Crull, Dallmann, Rev. Luther M. Wagner (1851–1930), Prof. August L. Graebner (1849–1904) of Concordia Seminary, and Rev. Frederick G. Kuegele, president of the English Synod. This committee was also charged with providing appropriate orders of worship for the hymnal.[59]

Figure 12: August Crull, circa 1885.

A month later, Crull wrote Dallmann, responding to a draft for an order of service that Dallmann had drawn up for the hymnal: "From now on, it appears to me that work prepared by you will not exactly be a happy occasion. (Please forgive me—that I so candidly and directly say what I mean!)." Crull chided the younger Dallmann for having "prepared an order of service according to none of the existing agendas . . ." and strongly urged "that one of the available good orders of service, as for example, the 'Common Service' or the one in the 'Church Book,' by and large, be

---

[58] "Proceedings of the First Convention of the General English Ev. Lutheran Conference of Missouri and Other States" (St. Louis, October 19–23, 1888), 14. Emphasis not original.

[59] Ibid., 16–17. See also A.[ugust L.] G.[raebner], "Die Allgemeine englisch-lutherisch Conferenz von Missouri und anderen Staaten," *Lehre und Wehre* 34, no. 11–12 (1888): 24 noted: "Ein anderes werthvolles Geschenk, das ihr von Professor A. Crull in Fort Wayne verehrt worden ist, das Manuscript eines englischen Kirchengesangbuchs, wurde einer Committee überwiesen, die zunächst eine Probedruck veranstalten soll. Auch ein Gottesdienstordnung soll dem Gesangbuch einverleibt werden."

retained."⁶⁰ *ELHB* 1889 eventually included Dallmann's *de novo* ordo, about which Dallmann would decades later admit to Walter Buszin that he was ". . . goaded to it by 'friends.' It was neither fish, flesh, nor fowl, nor Truman's good red herring."⁶¹ However, the second edition of *ELHB* in 1892 would eventually replace Dallmann's ordo with orders of service from the Common Service project prepared by the General Council, General Synod, and United Synod of the South.⁶²

By the end of November 1888, Crull reports that, "after a tremendous amount of work," he has finally forwarded "the manuscript of the English Hymnal 'cut and dried'" to Pastor Wagner, the second

---

⁶⁰ August Crull to William Dallmann, November 19, 1888, August Crull Collection, CHI, St. Louis, Missouri. "Sodann scheint mir die von Ihnen gefertigte Arbeit nicht gerade eine glückliche zu sein. (Verzeihen Sie mir gütigst, daß ich offen und gerade heraus sage, was ich meine!) Sie haben sich nämlich, wenn ich nicht sehr irre, nach keiner der vorhandenen Agenden genau gerichtet, sondern zu den bereits vorhandenen Ordnungen noch eine neue hinzugefügt: doch ist die Ordnung für 'Morning Service' allerdings fast ganz nach unser deutschen Mo. Agende eingerichtet. Auch in diesem Punkte stimme ich mehr mit P. Bartholomew als mit Ihnen. Ich würde, falls ich der Recht hätte, meine Meinung Ausdruck zu geben, ganz entschieden raten, eine der vorhandenen guten Ordnungen, wie z. B. die des 'Common Service,' oder die des 'Church Book,' im großen und ganzen beizubehalten und nur einzelne Stücke, wie etwa 'Absolution' und 'Spendeformel,' vielleicht auch etwas unnötiges und überflüssiges Zubehör abändern. Ich denke mir, das würde auch wohl Dr. Luther in einem ähnlichen Falle gethan haben, wenigstens läßt mich sein sonst so *konservatives* Verhalten das vermuten." Emphasis original.

⁶¹ William Dallmann to Walter E. Buszin, December 13, 1948, Walter E. Buszin Collection, CHI, St. Louis, Missouri.

⁶² The story of the development of the Common Service materials of 1888 is told most fabulously in Luther D. Reed, *The Lutheran Liturgy: A Study of the Common Liturgy of the Lutheran Church in America* (Philadelphia: Muhlenberg Press, 1959). The English Synod's adoption of the Common Service materials would eventually provide the Missouri Synod with English-language liturgical texts and orders of service in common with the majority of North American Lutheranism in the early twentieth century. For a study of sources of music used with these texts in the Missouri tradition, see James L. Brauer, "Trusty Steed or Trojan Horse? The Common Service in the *Evangelical Lutheran Hymn-Book,*" *Logia: A Journal of Lutheran Theology* 14, no. 3 (Holy Trinity 2005): 21–30.

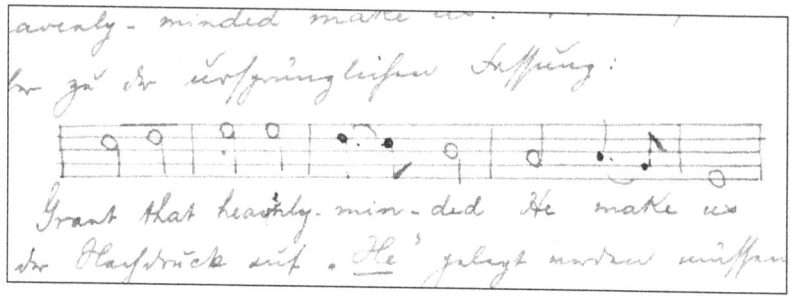

Figure 13: Crull's new word order for "Gott sei gelobet."

member of the committee, for review.[63] The following February, however, Crull reports to Dallmann via postcard that: "My manuscript has lain for four weeks in the study of Prof. G.[raebner, the next member of the committee to review it], who, in spite of all requests to hurry himself up, appears to be deaf. I wash my hands in innocence."[64]

By March 1889, the manuscript seems to have made its way out of Graebner's study and into the hands of Pastor Kuegele, the final member of the committee, who is reported by Crull to have recommended several untenable textual changes to the manuscript. The first involves Richard Massie's translation of "Gott sei gelobet," where Kuegele desires a different word order for one line. Crull points out that Kuegele's suggestion would be contrary to the meter (i.e., the way the words fall in relation to the music), and then Crull even sketches in the line of music to show what he means. (See Figure 13.) On another hymn, Massie's translation of Luther's "Vom Himmel hoch," Kuegele, a native English speaker serving as pastor in Virginia, remarks

---

[63] August Crull to William Dallmann, November 28, 1888, August Crull Collection, CHI, St. Louis, Missouri. "Habe nun heute endlich, nach allerdings riesiger Arbeit, das Ms. des engl. Gsgbchs fix u. fertig (cut and dried) Hrn. P. Wagner als dem *zweiten* Glied des Komitees zur Durchsicht übersandt. *Mich* trifft also in Zukunft der Vorwurf der Verzögerung *nicht*. Auch Ihren Entwurf (Order of D. S.) habe ich an genannten Herrn geschickt, mit der Bemerkung, daß ich persönlich die Benutzung der Ordnung des Council u. der Gen. Syn., mit geringen Abänderungen, befürworten würde." Emphasis original.

[64] August Crull to William Dallmann, February 11, 1889, August Crull Collection, CHI, St. Louis, Missouri. "Mein Ms. liegt nun seit ca. 4 Wochen im Studierzimmer des Hrn. Prof. G., der gegen alle Aufforderungen, sich zu beeilen, taub zu sein scheint. Ich wasche meine Hände in Unschuld."

that: "The word 'ass' is always embarrassing, even when it occurs in the Bible." While Crull doesn't necessarily agree with Kuegele's observations, he suggests a skilled modification of a Winkworth translation to resolve the issue:

Massie's Translation:
That Thou must lie on course dry grass,
The food of humble ox and ass.

Winkworth's Translation:
That Thou must choose Thy infant bed
Where ass and ox but lately fed!

Crull's Solution:
That Thou must choose Thy infant bed,
Where humble cattle lately fed.

Crull concludes: "You can see where I have lightly altered the translation by 'W.'[inkworth] . . . and have thereby gotten rid of the nefarious 'ass.'" Finally, Crull suggests a solution of his own to a minor issue Kuegele raises with a Massie translation of "Gelobet seist du, Jesu Christ."[65]

---

[65] August Crull to William Dallmann, March 29, 1889, August Crull Collection, CHI, St. Louis, Missouri. "Da Hr. P. Kuegele mich aufgefordert hat, hinsichtlich einiger Änderungen des Gesangbuch-Ms. an Sie zu berichten, erlaube ich mir, Ihnen folgende Mitteilungen zu machen.

1) Die von P. Kuegele gemachte Änderung in No. 186. III 6 muß getilgt werden, da sie unrichtig ist. Er hat offenbar ein ganz anderes Versmaß vorausgesetzt, als er änderte: Grant that He heavenly-minded make us! Versmaß und Melodie nötigen aber zu der ursprünglichen Fassung: [see Figure 13 for musical passage.] Sonst würde der Nachdruck auf 'He' gelegt werden müssen, während er doch auf 'heavenly-minded' liegt.

2) In No. 22 IX 3.4 wünscht P. K. eine Änderung. Er behauptet: 'The word "ass" is always embarrassing, even when it occurs in the Bible.' Obgleich ich nun diese Ansicht nicht teile, will ich doch den Druck nicht aufhalten und bitte Sie deshalb, statt der Übersetzung von Massie: 'that Thou must lie on coarse dry grass, The food of humble ox and ass,' die folgende, leise geänderte Übersetzung der Miss Winkworth zu setzen, die sich auch im Ohio Hymnal findet: 'That Thou must choose thy infant bed Where humble cattle lately fed.'

From March to July 1889, no letters have survived, and the first edition of *ELHB* 1889 went to the printer in Baltimore during this time.[66] All of the work that Crull had poured into the compilation of some 200 German translations and 200 original English-language hymn texts was finally put into print. Fortunately, there is a letter from Crull to Dallmann upon Crull's receipt of a copy of the first printing:

> Yesterday, I received from Mr. Treide a sample of the new English hymnal and was nearly scared to death as I began to examine it. Such shoddy workmanship I haven't seen in my entire life. The printer didn't use a consistent type throughout, but rather at one point used Brevier, at another Long Primer, and both seeded throughout each other. The proofreader, on the other hand (if there even was one), didn't understand his work at all. The most obvious and annoying errors still stand, as, for example, "Man of *Margareth*" in the place of "Nazareth," etc. The book positively swarms with such errors. On some fifty pages I found no fewer than 200 typos. In short, I, for one, would feel justified with all seriousness in protesting against the sale and distribution of such shoddy workmanship. Since this is not first-class, as the contract stipulated, the job should not be accepted—although I do pity the poor printer. At least we should make it impossible for such shoddy stuff to make us a laughingstock before all the world. The well-being

---

Sie sehen, so habe ich die Übersetzung der W. 'Where ox and ass but lately fed' leise geändert in: 'humble cattle' und bin somit den hinterstelligen 'ass' los geworden. Endlich 3) wünscht P. K. eine Änderung in No. 18. III 1.2. Er sagt nicht, weshalb, doch glaube ich, mißfällt ihm Massie's Ausdrück 'inwrap.' Auch hier sehe ich freilich keinen triftigen Grund zu feilen, allein ich will in der Sache nicht aufhalten und bitte Sie deshalb zu setzen:

'He whom the world could not inclose
Doth in Mary's lap repose.'

Hoffentlich ist's nun des Änderns genug!"

[66] In June 1889, Frederick Kuegele, "Notice," *Lutheran Witness* 8, no. 2 (1889): 16, wrote: "We take pleasure in making the announcement that our new hymn book will be ready for distribution by the end of June. The price has been fixed at 75 cents per copy or $8.00 per dozen. . . . We trust the brethren will use their best endeavors to give the book a wide distribution."

> **189** L. M.
>
> BEHOLD, a stranger's at the door!
> He gently knocks, has knocked before,
> Has waited long, is waiting still;
> You treat no other friend so ill.
>
> 2 But will He prove a friend indeed?
> He will; the very friend you need;
> The Man of Margareth, 't is He,
> With garments dyed at Calvary.

Figure 14: "Man of Margareth" (stanza 2, line 3), one of the many typos in ELHB *1889.*

of our congregations and the honor of our church must stand for us higher than the well-being (that is, the money bags) of certain parishioners. Therefore, I would not accept the job, but rather refuse it.

This turn of events pains me to no end—that my work has been so badly mutilated; and even worse, that the congregations of our Synod should have to wait now even longer for a hymnal. There can be no other way, since it is out of the question for us to give them such garbage.[67]

---

[67] August Crull to William Dallmann, August 13, 1889, August Crull Collection, CHI, St. Louis, Missouri. "Gestern erhielt ich durch Hrn. Treide ein Exemplar des neuen engl. Gesangbuchs und erschrak fast zum Tode, als ich es einigermaßen prüfte. Ein so hundsmiserables Machwerk habe ich in meinem ganzen Leben noch nicht gesehen. Der Drucker hat ja nicht einmal reine Typen gebraucht, sondern bald Brevier, bald Long Primer, bald beides brut durcheinander. Der Korrektor aber, wenn ein solcher überhaupt thätig war, hat seine Arbeit gar nicht verstanden: die gröbsten, sinnstörendsten Fehler sind stehen geblieben, wie z. B. Man of *Margareth* statt Nazareth etc. Das Buch wimmelt förmlich von solchen Fehlern; auf ca. 50 Seiten habe ich wenigstens 200 Druckfehler gefunden. Kurz, ich für meinen Person glaube mich berechtigt, allen Ernstes gegen den Verkauf und die Verbreitung eines solchen Schund-Machwerks zu protestieren. Der Job, weil nicht first class, wie der Kontrakt es fordert, sollte nicht acceptiert werden, obwohl der arme Drucker mich dauert; allein wir

An examination of the first printing of the *ELHB* would suggest that Crull's observations regarding the printing problems appear to be justified.[68] In October of that year, President Kuegele wrote in *Der Lutheraner* regarding the first printing:

> The printing mistakes which one finds should not in any way hinder the examination of this book. They are to be eliminated in the thousand copies which are still unbound.[69]

It appears that these printing mistakes were eventually "eliminated" in the remaining thousand copies by the inclusion of a sheet titled "Corrections" pasted on the inside the front cover.[70]

At the May 1891 convention of the English Synod, a report on "Business Matters" acknowledged: "The Hymn Book has produced a rather mixed impression."[71] President Kuegele also noted in his report:

> An edition of 2000 copies of our Hymnbook was published,

> dürfen uns unmöglich mit einem solchen Schund vor der ganzen Welt lächerlich machen. Das Wohl unsrer Gemeinden und die Ehre unsrer Kirche muß uns höher stehen als das Wohl (d.i. der Geldsack) eines Gemeindeglieds. Darum würde ich den Job nicht annehmen, sondern refüsieren. Unendlich leid thut mir dies Schicksal, das meine Arbeit getroffen hat; noch mehr leid aber, daß die Gemeinden unseres Verbandes noch länger auf ein Gesangbuch warten sollen; allein es geht doch nicht anders, denn solchen Schund dürfen wir ihnen unmöglich bieten." Emphasis original.

[68] An announcement in the *Lutheran Witness* of recent publications made no mention of the printing problems, noting instead that ". . . this book contains the very cream of our German church-songs and the very marrow of what constitutes [English-language] hymnals of American Churches." "Review of *Evangelical Lutheran Hymn Book*," *Lutheran Witness* 8, no. 6 (1889): 48.

[69] F.[rederick] Kügele, "Englisches Gesangbuch," *Der Lutheraner* 45 (October 8, 1889): 166; as translated in Carl Schalk, *The Roots of Hymnody in The Lutheran Church—Missouri Synod*, no. 2, Church Music Pamphlet Series (St. Louis: Concordia Publishing House, 1965), 42.

[70] One of two surviving copies of *ELHB* 1889 at CHI, St. Louis contains such a pasted list of corrections on the inside front cover of what appears to be its original binding.

[71] "Proceedings of the Second Convention of the English Evangelical Lutheran Synod of Missouri and Other States" (St. Louis, May 20–26, 1891), 35.

> and the entire edition has been sold. It is therefore incumbent on Conference to make provision for the publishing of a second edition. In this connection I would remark that the thanks of Conference are due to various gentlemen who contributed funds, as also to Prof. A. Crull of Fort Wayne, for assistance rendered in the publishing of the book.[72]

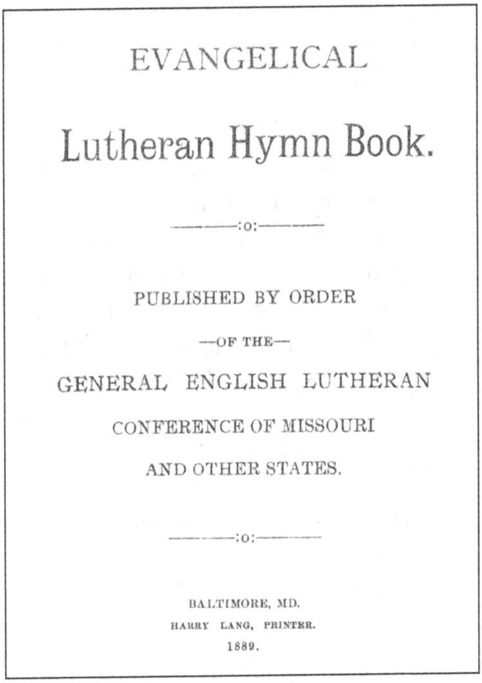
EVANGELICAL

Lutheran Hymn Book.

———:o:———

PUBLISHED BY ORDER

—OF THE—

GENERAL ENGLISH LUTHERAN

CONFERENCE OF MISSOURI

AND OTHER STATES.

———:o:———

BALTIMORE, MD.

HARRY LANG, PRINTER.

1889.

Figure 15: Title page to ELHB *1889.*

When it came time for action, however, the Synod resolved to appoint a new committee of four, with only two from the previous committee—Dallmann and Kuegele (by default as President of Synod). In other words, Crull was *not* reappointed. The new committee was charged

> to consult with others and their work defined thus,—to correct defective translations that are wanting in meter or in wording, to drop those that never will be sung and replace them by others, and to add good new hymns which had been overlooked in the first edition.

Provisions were also made to inquire with the General Council and the United Synod of the South regarding the possibility of including the "Common Service for Morning and Evening without mattings [sic]."[73]

Three months after the convention, it appears that Dallmann exercised the provision to "consult with others" in the work of the com-

72 Ibid., 8–9.

73 Ibid., 37.

mittee by asking Crull for his assistance. Crull's response from Manitou Springs, Colorado, however, demonstrates the emotional toll this project had taken on him:

> Yesterday I finally received your lines from the 6th which were forwarded to me here where, at the advice of the doctors on account of my shattered health, I am taking a break. Shortly after I last saw you, I had a breakdown; the doctor called the affliction "nervous prostration," compounded with a persistent throat ailment. I've been here now for fourteen days without feeling any real improvement. Under these circumstances you will find it understandable as to why I haven't been able yet to do anything with the English hymnal, and so I leave any changes to the text or contents to your discretion. I certainly don't have any authority, yet alone any say so, and therefore no further responsibility. I am very happy that you were successful in acquiring the Common Service. At least this part of the hymnal will be good, in spite of the many defects that stand out in the part that I prepared.[74]

Crull's "breakdown" and the diagnosis of "nervous prostration" notwithstanding,[75] at this point he appears to have wanted little or

---

[74] August Crull to William Dallmann, August 24, 1891, August Crull Collection, CHI, St. Louis, Missouri. "Gestern endlich erhielt ich Ihre Zeilen vom 6. dss, welche mir hieher nachgeschickt wurden, wo ich mich auf Rat der Ärzte wegen meiner zerrütteten Gesundheit eine Zeitlang aufhalten soll. Bald nachdem ich Sie zuletzt gesehen hatte, brach ich zusammen; die Arzt nennt das Leiden nervous prostration, verbunden mit einer hartnäckigen Halsaffection. Ich bin nun 14 Tage lang hier, ohne bisher wesentliche Besserung zu spüren. Unter diesen Umständen werden Sie es erklärlich finden, wenn ich für das engl. Gesangbuch nichts gethan habe noch thun kann, sondern jedweder Veränderung des Textes, sowie des Inhalts Ihrem Ermessen anheimstelle. Ich habe ja auch keinerlei Recht, fernerhin ein Wörtchen drein zu reden, und somit dann auch keinerlei Verantwortlichkeit mehr. — Herzlich freut mich, daß es Ihnen gelungen ist, das Common Service zu erlangen. Dieser Teil des Gesangbuches wird wenigstens gut sein, soviel Mängel auf dem von mir ausgearbeiteten Teil desselben ankleben mögen."

[75] John F. McDermott, "Emily Dickinson's 'Nervous Prostration' and Its Possible Relationship to Her Work," *The Emily Dickinson Journal* 9, no. 1 (Spring 2000): 71–86, notes concerning the diagnosis of "nervous

nothing to do with the new committee's work on *ELHB* 1892, and there is no evidence to suggest that he ever did. Thus, the committee went on without him: 1) retaining the original 400 hymns of *ELHB* 1889 (with the same assigned hymn numbers); 2) swapping in a few alternate translations for a handful of the German hymns; 3) adding an additional fifty hymns in an appendix at the end (hymns 401–450); and 4) swapping in the Common Service orders for the poorly-received Dallmann creation.[76]

---

prostration" toward the end of the nineteenth century: "It included many symptoms, such as profound exhaustion, insomnia, pressure and heaviness in the head, palpitation of the heart, trembling of the muscles, as well as multiple fears, including fears "of open places or closed places, fear of society, fear of being alone . . ." At least in the case of Emily Dickinson, it appears to have included bouts with acute anxiety and severe depression.

It appears that Crull may have struggled with some form of severe depression or disorder at other points in his life as well. In addition to his 1866 sabbatical to Germany and his "breakdown" in 1891, there is also a letter from June 8, 1881 from C. F. W. Walther to a member of the Board of Regents for Concordia College, Fort Wayne, where Crull served as professor, noting that "Prof. Crull, for his part, instead of being able to recover and recuperate here [at Walther's home], rather became more run down than he was when he arrived. . . ." Walther implores the Board of Regents not to insist that Crull continue to function the remaining weeks of the semester. See C. F. W. Walther, *Selected Letters* (St. Louis: Concordia Publishing House, 1981), 164–65. In 1915, Crull resigned from his service at Concordia College due to health reasons and was later committed to a sanitarium in Milwaukee by his family. There is a lengthy, first-hand account by Professor Otto F. Hattstaedt, the only pastor who was allowed to visit him while he was in the hospital, and it indicates that, during those dark days, Crull believed he had lost his faith and that he was therefore abandoned by God. See Otto F. Hattstaedt, "The Distress of the Sainted Prof. August Crull," n.d., August Crull Collection, CHI, St. Louis, Missouri.

76 William Dallmann, "The New Hymn Book Contains," *Lutheran Witness* 10, no. 19 (1892): 149. In addition, Dallmann notes: "The characteristic feature that makes this book superior to all other English Lutheran hymn books is the large number—over two hundred—of the beautiful German Lutheran chorals [sic] given in it in translations according to the original meter and without mutilation by arbitrary abbreviation. . . ."

In March 1892, Crull writes Dallmann thanking him for a copy of the second edition, and declining, yet again, an invitation to review the hymnal. But this time, Crull cannot entirely restrain himself and continues further:

> A quick browse through the book drew my attention to several of what I take to be obvious blunders . . .
>
> 2) [John] Kelly's version of the [Gerhardt] hymn, "O Welt, sieh hier dein Leben." How you could have included such a dismal production, which in grammatical as well as metrical respects exhibits so many obvious blunders, is absolutely inexplicable to me. The mere agreement of the meter with the original does not justify the inclusion of such incompetence. For example, "und das betrübte *Marterheer*," ["and the afflicted host of agonies"] Kelly fouls up with: "And the afflicted *martyr host*"! . . .
>
> Furthermore, 3) So many hymns in the Appendix, which were not written to the tunes of church hymns, therefore do not belong in a church hymnal, e.g., "I Am Jesus' Little Lamb," "Jesus, Lead Thou On," and others. And the most displeasing to me in this section is the burial hymn, "Why Do We Mourn" [by Isaac Watts] with the colossal absurdity, "Where should the dying members rest but with the *dying Head*?" You must certainly have included this hymn only to please your learned co-worker [Pastor] Wagner, who earlier pestered me with this and other similar foolishness.
>
> Well, "facta infecta fieri non possunt" ["What's done can't be undone"], so I'll just shut up, especially since it won't get any better as the result of any arguments I might make. . . .[77]

---

[77] August Crull to William Dallmann, March 21, 1892, August Crull Collection, CHI, St. Louis, Missouri. "Ein flüchtiges Durchblättern des Buches hat mich freilich mancherlei sehen lassen, was ich für offenbare Missgriffe halte. . . . Dahin gehört 2) die Kelly'sche Version des Liedes: 'O Welt, sieh hier dein Leben.' Wie Sie ein so trauriges Produkt, das in sprachlicher wie in metrischer Hinsicht so viele grobe Schnitzer aufweist, haben auf[weise]nehmen können, ist mir schlechterdings unerklärlich. Denn die blosse Uebereinstimmung des Metrums mit dem Original [be]recht[fer]tigt die Aufnahme einer solchen Stümperei doch sicherlich nicht.

The bitter pill of the printing errors in the first edition, along with his official exclusion from the committee for the second edition, appear to have shaped the rhetoric that Crull employs and color his criticisms of the new committee's work from this point forward. In two remaining letters, written just over a week apart toward the end of November 1892, Crull continues his criticism of the second edition of *ELHB*, picking up where he had left off several months earlier:

1) No. 77, the truly *scandalous* blunder of the hymn "O Welt, sieh hier, etc.," which J.[ohn] Kelly has brought to ruin. I will remain silent about "the afflicted martyr host" ("der betrübten Marterheer") and only point you to the pseudo-English, which, "like a golden strand," runs throughout the entire so-called translation . . . If this isn't "murdering the King's English," then I give up![78]

A week later, Crull writes his final exchange with Dallmann, apparently responding to a number of issues from a previous letter that no longer survives:

Z.B. 'und das betrübte *Marterheer*' verhunzt Kelly in: 'And the afflicted martyr host'! . . . Dahin gehören 3) so manch Lieder im Appendix, die nicht Tone des Kirchenliedes gedichtet sind und deshalb auch nicht in ein Kirchengesangbuch gehören, z.B. 'Weil ich Jesu Schäflein bin'; 'Jesu, geh voran' u.a. Am meisten misfällt mir unter diesen freilich das Grablied 'Why do we mourn' mit dem kolossalen Unsinn: 'Where should the dying members rest, but with the *dying Head*?' Doch dieses Lied mussten Sie jedenfalls Ihrem gelehrten Mitarbeiter Wagner zuliebe aufnehmen, der mich früher mit diese[n]r und ählichen Albernheiten drangsalierte. Nun 'facta infecta fieri non possunt:' ergo will ich das Maul halten, zumal da ja doch nichts mit dem Räsonnieren gebessert wird. . . ." Emphasis original.

[78] August Crull to William Dallmann, November 22, 1892, August Crull Collection, CHI, St. Louis, Missouri. "1). No. 77. die wahrhafts *himmelschreiende* Verhunzung des Liedes: 'O Welt, sieh hier etc,' die sich J. Kelly hat zu Schulden kommen lassen. Ich will schweigen von 'the afflicted martyr host' (der betrübten Marter-heer) und Sie nur hinweisen auf die [uncertain]englische Sprache, die sich 'wie ein goldener (!) Faden' durch die ganze sog. Übersetzung hindurchsicht . . . Wenn das nicht "murdering the King's English" ist, dann verzichte ich auf jegliches Urteil." Emphasis original.

To my sorrow, I feel compelled to go on the defensive. As you will recall, you asked me, for the purpose of printing a new edition of the hymnal, to be attentive to any defects that may have arisen, and after having done this with my usual candor, I see that I have entangled myself in a controversy. Right now, though, quite frankly, I'm just about out of not only passion, but also of time and energy to engage in such a task, since I also have a ton of work to do on an assignment from Synod to develop the draft of a grammar for high school students. But since I have already said "A," I must now also say "B"—as briefly and succinctly as possible.

If I was not entirely successful in stating the problem with Kelly's translation of the two hymns, then I wouldn't waste another word on this matter. There are, of course, various other translations that are not entirely successful—for example, those prepared by myself, as *I* am most acutely aware. However, I must characterize the existing translations, in spoken language, to be downright bad, and neither grammatically nor poetically justifiable. I do not believe it is too much to claim when I dubbed the broken English in these hymns to be downright "scandalous." Had *I* been in your place, if I could not have dispensed with the synodical resolution in this case nor been able myself to provide an improved translation, I would have scrapped the two hymns rather than spoil the hymnal with such caricatures. Just consider "the afflicted *martyr host*"! That's just about as bad as "the man of Margareth"! I already have a literal "translation" of the hymn "O welt, sieh hier etc." by Jacobi,[79] but it is quite possibly even worse than the one by Kelly. Therefore, there doesn't remain anything else to do but to prepare a new one. For *me* alone the assignment is too difficult; I could, with the best stretch of the imagination, bring it off if I had the necessary time and passion. But this also fails me until the current circumstances are completely concluded. . . .

---

[79] As keeper of the Royal German Chapel in St. James' Palace, London, John Christian Jacobi (1670–1750) translated a number of German hymns for eighteenth-century British royalty. See Raymond F. Glover, ed., *The Hymnal 1982 Companion,* 3 vols. in 4 (New York: The Church Hymnal Corporation, 1994), 2:487–88.

4) I'm not budging in reference to stanza 4 of No. 449 ["Why Do We Mourn Departing Friends" by Isaac Watts]. The other hymns you cite will also not pacify me on this point . . . For once, I would just like to see the pertinent words translated [into German]. After the poet has very nicely said that the Lord, through his lying in the grave, has sanctified and blessed the graves of his saints, he continues [here Crull translates Watt's English into German]: "Where else should the dying members rest than with the dying Head?" He apparently wants to say that the members of Christ (that is, his Christians) after death should rest there where once also his head (that is, Christ's head) rested after his death—namely, in the grave. However, unfortunately, he does not say that. He speaks of the *dying* head; that, however, gives us nothing more. Christ *was* dead, but now he is living. The dying Head hung on the *cross*. Is that where the dying members should rest? In short, the thoughts of the poet are much too pale and indefinite—so much so that I by no such authority can determine to call it beautiful or edifying, or to commend it to Lutheran Christians to sing.

So now, I probably should and certainly do want to conclude. I'm happy that *I* don't have any culpability with regard to this matter and am not bound through any such "synodical resolution" as you are. Above all, I am reminded of your current place between Scylla and Charybdis. I am truly sorry that I can do nothing to free you from them.[80]

---

[80] August Crull to William Dallmann, December 1, 1892, August Crull Collection, CHI, St. Louis, Missouri. "Zu meinem Bedauern sehe ich mich genötigt, die Defensive zu ergreifen. Wie sie sich erinnern werden, hatten Sie mich gebeten, Sie behufs einer neuen Auflage des Gesangbuchs auf etwaige Mängel aufmerksam zu machen, und nachdem ich dies mit gewohnter Offenherzigkeit gethan habe, sehe ich mich in eine Kontroverse verwickelt. Dazu fehlt es mir aber, offen gestanden, nicht nur an Lust, sondern auch an Zeit und Kraft in Anspruch nimmt, auch an der mir von der Synode aufgetragenen Ausarbeitung einer Grammatik für höhere Schulen überreichlich zu tun habe. Doch da ich A gesagt, muss ich nun auch B sagen, aber so kurz und bündig als möglich.

Wenn ich mit Ihnen Kelly's Übersetzung der beiden Lieder nur 'nicht ganz gelungen' nenne könnte, so würde ich kein Wort weiter in dieser Sache verlieren. Sind doch auch noch mehrere der Übersetzungen nich ganz ge-

Crull was bitterly unhappy with where others had taken his work. Although he carefully explained the reasoning behind his objections to the translation by John Kelly and the hymn by Isaac Watts, his so-

> lungen, z.b. die von mir selbst angefertigten, wie *ich* das wohl am lebhaftesten fühle. Aber ich muss die in Rede stehenden Übersetzungen als geradezu *schlecht* bezeichnen, da sie weder sprachlich noch prosodisch zu rechtfertigen sind. Ich glaube nicht zu viel zu behaupten, wenn ich das Englisch, das in diesen Liedern verbrochen wird, geradezu *'himmelschreiend'* nenne. An Ihrer Stelle hätte *ich* deshalb, wenn ich mich von dem Synodalbeschluss in diesem Falle nicht hätte dispensieren, oder nicht selbst eine bessere Uebersetzung hätte liefern können, die beiden Lieder lieber geopfert, als dass ich das Gesangbuch mit solchen Karrikaturen verunziert hätte. Denken Sie nur an 'the afflicted *martyr host'*! Das ist beinahe ebenso schlimm wie *'the Man of Margaret'*! – Ich habe noch eine wortgetreue 'Uebersetzung' des Liedes: 'O Welt, sieh hier u.s.w.' von Jacobi, aber dies ist womöglich noch schlechter als die von Kelly. Somit bleibe wohl nichts anderes übrig al seine neue anzufertigen. Allein *mir* ist die Aufgabe zu schwer; ich könnte es beim besten Willen nicht zustande bringen, selbst wenn ich die nötige Zeit und Lust dazu hätte, und auch daran fehlt es mir unter den jetzigen Umständen ganz entschieden. . . .
>
> 4. Gerade so stehe ich in betreff der 4. Str. in No. 449. Auch die anderen Gesangbücher können mich über diesen Punkt nicht beruhigen . . . Wir wollen die betreffenden Worte einmal übersetzen. Nachdem der Dichter schön gesagt hat, dass der Herr durch sein Liegen in Grabe der Gräber seiner Heiligen geheiligt und gesegnet habe, fährt er fort: 'Wo sonst sollten die sterbenden Glieder rühen als bei dem sterbenden Haupt?' Er will offenbar sagen, dass die Glieder des Herrn, seine Christen, nach dem Tode da ruhen sollen, wo einst auch ihr Haupt, Christus, nach seinem Tode geruht hat, nämlich im Grabe; aber leider sagt er das nicht. Er redet von dem *sterbenden* Haupt; das aber giebt es nicht mehr. Es *war* tod, aber ist lebendig. Das *sterbende* Haupt hat aber nicht im *Grabe* gelegen, sondern das *tote* Haupt. Das sterbende Haupt hing am *Kreuze*. Da sollen die sterbenden Glieder doch nicht ruhen? Kurz, der Gedanke des Dichters ist mir viel zu blass und unbestimmt, als dass ich mich durch irgend welche Autoritäten bestimmen lassen könnte, ihn schön oder erbaulich zu nennen und ihn den lutherischen Christen zu Singen zu empfehlen.
>
> Doch nun muss und will ich schließen. Ich freue mich, dass *ich* in dieser Angelegenheit keine Verantwortlichkeit habe und nicht durch einen *'Synodalbeschluss'* gebunden bin wie Sie. Denn allerdings erinnert Ihre jetzige Lage an Scylla und Charybdis. Es thut mir darum hertzlich leid, dass ich Sie nicht aus derselben befreien kann." Emphasis original.

lution—to scrap the two hymns completely—was apparently not a viable option for Dallmann and his committee, especially since the second edition had been printed and the committee had therefore already executed its mandate. It is interesting, however, that when the *ELHB* underwent its final revision in the form of *ELHB* 1912, Kelly's mistranslation of Gerhardt's "der betrübten Marterheer" was, indeed, corrected to: "And with afflictions' scourging host."[81] Watts' burial hymn, however, was retained—complete with "Where should the dying members rest / But with their dying Head?"[82] Apparently, a blatant mistranslation was one thing, poetic license quite another.

Although August Crull was the singular architect and visionary for the hymnody in *ELHB* 1889, the precise implementation of his vision was left in the hands of others. His "valuable gift" of *ELHB* 1889 to the English Synod was gratefully received, but it consequently became the property of revision committees, synodical conventions, and the larger church. Nevertheless, the hymnal he provided would serve a generation of English-speaking Missourians and would ultimately form the foundation for all Missouri Synod hymnals to follow.

The Long Journey toward ELHB *1912*

The twenty-year journey from *ELHB* 1892 to its final revision in *ELHB* 1912 was long and tortuous, with a number of starts and stops along the way. It began already at the 1891 convention of the English Synod when a motion was made to insert the tunes of the hymns in the forthcoming *ELHB* 1892. The synod chose not to go in this direction, but rather to appoint a committee to deliberate the publication of a separate "Tune Book."[83] Thus, the journey toward *ELHB* 1912 began as a quest for a tune book to be used in concert with *ELHB* 1892.[84]

---

[81] *ELHB* 1912, no. 205.

[82] Ibid., no. 542.

[83] "Proceedings of the Second Convention of the English Evangelical Lutheran Synod of Missouri and Other States," in St. Louis, 1891 (Baltimore: Harry Lang), 37. Tune Book Committee members appointed were "Revs. O. M. Kaiser, Th. Huegli, and A. S. Bartholomew."

[84] The publication of separate text and tune editions was in keeping with the practice of German Missouri, where *KELG* 1847 and its successive editions were printed as text-only for congregational use. The organist,

At the 1893 convention of the English Synod, the Tune Book Committee recommended that the synod defer indefinitely the publication of its own tune book. "It was stated that Layriz's Choralbuch,[85] 'Church Song,'[86] The Common Service by Mrs. H. Krauth,[87] were sufficient to find the tunes for all the hymns contained in our hymnal."[88] This recommendation was accepted by the convention, but the call for a comprehensive tune book for *ELHB* 1892 did not go away. Four years later, the English Synod received another request to produce a tune book for *ELHB* 1892 and resolved to consider that possibility in light of a potential revision of their hymnal. The Revision Committee was given the task to assess the need and report to the next convention.[89]

then, had the responsibility of locating an appropriate accompaniment in other published sources. For more on the various tune editions available to organists during this period, see Schalk, *God's Song in a New Land*, 131–32.

[85] Most likely this would have been one of the later editions of Layriz's harmonizations published to go with *KELG*, either H. F. Hoelter, ed. *Choralbuch: Eine Sammlung der gangbarsten Choräle der evang.-lutherischen Kirche, meist Dr. Fr. Layriz nebst den wichtigsten Sätzen* (St. Louis: Concordia Publishing House, 1886); or, Karl Brauer, ed. *Mehrstimmiges Choralbuch zu dem "Kirchengesangbuch für Evangelisch-Lutherische Gemeinden Ungeänderter Augsburgischer Confession"* (St. Louis: Concordia Publishing House, 1888).

[86] Joseph Augustus Seiss and Charles Pilling Engelmann, eds., *Church Song* (Philadelphia: Lutheran Book Store, 1875).

[87] Harriet Reynolds Krauth, ed. *Church Book for the Use of Evangelical Lutheran Congregations* (Philadelphia: J. K. Shryock, 1893). First published in 1891, this volume was a revision of the tune edition to all the hymns of the General Council's *CB* 1868, with the addition of the music for the Common Service. See Schalk, *God's Song in a New Land*, 145.

[88] "Proceedings of the Third Convention of the English Evangelical Lutheran Synod of Missouri and Other States," in Chicago, 1893 (Baltimore: Lutheran Publication Board), 36.

[89] "Proceedings of the Fifth Convention of the English Evangelical Lutheran Synod of Missouri and Other States," in Baltimore, 1897 (Pittsburgh: American Lutheran Publication Board), 39–40. Members of the Revision Committee at this time were William Dallmann, Adolf W. Meyer (1860–1937), and Frederick Kuegele. The Revision Committee was generally responsible for making recommendations to the Publication Board regarding new publications and revisions of existing publications. It also

At the 1899 convention, the American Lutheran Publication Board (the publishing arm of the English Synod) reported that the printings of *ELHB* continued to experience "a regular sale"—so much so that the board "begs leave herewith to inform the honorable Synod of the wearing of the plates of our Hymn Book." Yet, in light of pending revisions to the hymnal, the board urged that any revisions to be included be determined *before* new plates were ordered.[90] The floor committee that received this report therefore recommended that "a Committee be appointed to thoroughly revise the Hymn Book both as to contents and form, said Committee to report to the next convention."[91]

On a second parallel track, the Revision Committee noted that "the revision of the Hymn Book has also been completed and the corrections and improvements suggested by us are herewith submitted to the judgment of Synod."[92] Yet, the floor committee that received this report recommended that "the old Revision Committee be appointed a special Committee for revising the Hymn Book, that this new Committee call for suggestions by publishing the plan thus far agreed on, in the *Lutheran Witness,* and that it give for suggestions 60 days' time, and that at the expiration of this term the Committee proceed at once to publish this work."[93]

Finally, on a third parallel track, the Tune Book Committee reported that "the list of tunes had been prepared, but advised Synod not to take further action until the revision of the Hymn Book had been completed." Their report was adopted, and it was furthermore

---

appears that the Revision Committee was responsible for doctrinal review of all published materials. A. W. Meyer, "Our Synod," *Lutheran Witness* 21, no. 7 (1902): 53, notes: ". . . our Synod jealously guards doctrinal purity, having created a Board of Revision, that is to examine all manuscripts, not otherwise provided for editorially by Synod. Our Synod considers it a duty to provide books and periodicals of an irreproachable character for her congregations."

[90] "Proceedings of the Sixth Convention of the English Evangelical Lutheran Synod of Missouri and Other States," in 1899 (Pittsburgh: American Lutheran Publication Board), 44.

[91] Ibid., 46. This action was tabled, however, pending the report of the Hymn Book Revision Committee.

[92] Ibid., 47.

[93] Ibid., 48.

resolved that the committee submit the manuscript to the Publication Board following a thirty-day vetting period in the *Lutheran Witness*.[94]

The confusion of parallel committees and their overlapping and even contradictory mandates came to a head at the 1901 convention when the standing committee on Revision of the Hymn-Book reported:

> 1. Owing to the fact that there was a good deal of unclearness as to what kind of a revision was desired, the committee did not think it wise to take any steps towards publishing a new edition of the hymn-book, until Synod shall have defined more definitely what kind of revision it desired.
>
> 2. Since the publishing of a tune book will necessitate the rearranging of the hymns of the present hymn-book and since, moreover, some of the hymns contained in it are unusable and some that are very desirable are missing, we commend a thorough revision, both as to form and contents.
>
> 3. We recommend that this present committee be dissolved and a new one be appointed that will be in a better position to do the work, and that this committee be instructed to present its manuscript at the next convention of Synod.
>
> 4. We recommend that, pending this thorough revision of the hymn-book, the Revision Committee be instructed to correct the printer's mistakes in the present edition and that these be then eliminated on the plates as far as practicable.

Synod adopted the recommendations of this report and combined the Revision of Hymn Book Committee and Committee on Tune Books into a single committee.[95] Prof. Louis Kahmer (1877–1963) of Peabody Conservatory, Baltimore had previously been appointed to work on harmonizations for the hymnal,[96] and only the musical set-

---

[94] Ibid., 48–49.

[95] "Proceedings of the Seventh Convention of the Evangelical Lutheran Synod of Missouri and Other States," in Buffalo, 1901 (Pittsburgh: American Lutheran Publication Board), 137–38. Members appointed to the new committee were: "Revs. Dallmann, Morhart, Hemmeter, Kaiser, Sachs, Detzer."

[96] Ibid., 14–15. Eventually Kahmer's musical settings of the orders of service were published in: Louis Kahmer, ed. *The Common Service with*

tings for the various services remained. A committee to gather funds for the publication of the new hymnal was also created.[97]

Lack of funding for the new hymnal appears to have further hampered progress between 1901 and 1903. At the 1903 Convention, the Publication Board reported that the expense of debuting the English Synod's *Sunday-School Hymnal* in 1901, as well as other capital outlays, made it impossible to move forward with publication of a revision to *ELHB* 1892.[98] Thus, the Publication Board recommended that in the future "Synod should devise some means of financing these expensive undertakings in such a manner as to avoid crippling the Publication Board in its office of financially aiding synod's treasury."[99]

At the 1905 Convention, the "Hymn-Book Revision and Tune-Book Committee" that had been appointed at the 1901 Convention provided a full report of their activities thus far. Most significantly, they reported that just one month prior to the convention, they had published in the *Lutheran Witness* "the list of tunes and hymns selected" for the revision of *ELHB* 1892.[100] Synod accepted their report and

---

Music (Pittsburgh: American Lutheran Publication Board, 1906).

[97] "Proceedings of the Seventh Convention of the Evangelical Lutheran Synod of Missouri and Other States," 61.

[98] "Proceedings of the Eighth Convention of the Evangelical Lutheran Synod of Missouri and Other States," in Pittsburgh, 1903 (Pittsburgh: American Lutheran Publication Board), 57–58, notes that 11,200 copies of *ELHB* were printed, and that 12,000 copies of *SSH* 1901 were printed during the 1901–03 biennium. Regarding the capital outlay to produce *SSH* 1901, "Proceedings of the Seventh Convention of the Evangelical Lutheran Synod of Missouri and Other States," 131, notes that the initial printing of *SSH* 1901 was 5,000 copies of the text-only edition, and 5,000 copies of the tune edition, and that: "The vast amount of labor such a publication entails will never be known by those who have escaped the experience. Nor will the cost. The determination to present to Synod at this session this book complete, was the cause of the concentration of all our energies, financial and others, upon this, in every way, expensive publication."

[99] "Proceedings of the Eighth Convention of the Evangelical Lutheran Synod of Missouri and Other States," 58.

[100] "Proceedings of the Ninth Convention of the Evangelical Lutheran Synod of Missouri and Other States," in St. Louis, 1905 (Pittsburgh: American Lutheran Publication Board), 66.

"adopted the new Hymn-book proposed by the committee with the provision that suggestions may be sent in; the committee, however, having full power to accept or reject them."[101] Furthermore, to avoid a financial crunch similar to the one experienced earlier with the publication of *SSH* 1901, the Hymn-Book Committee was also "made a committee of ways and means for the publication of the hymn-book." The convention resolved, therefore, "that the Committee go ahead with publishing the hymn-book only under the condition that it place no financial burden upon Synod."[102]

The list of hymn titles and assigned tunes published in the *Lutheran Witness* in June 1905 is most instructive. The article begins:

> The Hymn Book Committee presents for revision the following list of tunes and additional hymns for the proposed new edition of the hymn book. The numbers preceding the name of a tune refer to hymns in the present hymnal. The new hymns are given in first lines with tune. All suggestions should be addressed to the Secretary, p. t., C. C. Morhart, 228 Morgan Street, N. W., Washington, D. C.[103]

The article then lists 634 hymns—either by hymn number from *ELHB* 1892 or by title (if not already in *ELHB* 1892). Of the 634 hymns listed, 66 (10%) were never included in *ELHB* 1912. On the other hand, 26 hymns that had not been proposed in the 1905 article were eventually included among the 567 hymns that comprised *ELHB* 1912. This demonstrates that as early as 1905, the committee had already settled on some nine out of ten hymns to be included in the revision of their hymnal. This early dating of the committee's work is reinforced when one considers an additional feature of this article: the listing of hymn titles and tunes according to the thematic headings envisioned for the organization of the hymns in *ELHB* 1912.

But for a few minor exceptions, the headings included in *ELHB* 1912 were already established by the time of the 1905 article. And yet, a comparison of the similarities and differences in thematic headings between *ELHB* 1892 and *ELHB* 1912 is in-

---

[101] Ibid., 67.

[102] Ibid., 67.

[103] C. C. Morhart, "Hymns and Tunes for a New Hymnal," *Lutheran Witness* 24, no. 12 (1905): 91–93.

ARRANGEMENT OF HYMNS.

I Sunday	1- 14	
1 Opening 1.4.6.7.8.13.14.		
2 Closing 2.3.5.9.10.11.12.		
II Advent and Christmas	15- 40	
III New Year	41- 49	401
IV Epiphany	50- 52	402
V Presentation	53- 57	
VI Passion	58- 87	
VII Easter	88- 98	
VIII Ascension	99-108	
IX Pentecost	109-122	
X Trinity	123-131	
XI Michaelmas	132-134	
XII Reformation	135-138	403-404
IIIII The Word and the Church	139-170	405 412
1 Glory of the Word 142.148.149. 150.152.		
2 Power 163.169.		
3 Invitation 155.166.167.		
4 Cornerstone Laying 139.140.		
5 Dedication 146.147.159.		
6 Protection of 14..143.145.152.165. 168.1.0.412.		
7 Loyalty to 151.156.158.160.161.409. 410.		
8 Communion of Saints 157.411.		
9 Mission 144.154.162. 64.405.406.407 408.		
XIV Catechism	171-186	413-426
1 Ten Commandments 172.173.		
2 Creed 1.4.175.		
3 Prayer 176.413.		
4 Baptism 17.-179.414-417.		
5 Absolution 180. 181.		
6 Lord's Supper 182-186.418-426.		
XV Repentance	187-203	
XVI Faith and Justification	204-221	427-428

Figure 16: Excerpt from "Arrangement of Hymns" from ELHB 1892.

structive. In terms of similarities, the central role of the Church Year in *ELHB* 1912 is still strongly present in the first half of the hymnal; a few elaborations (e.g., "Circumcision," "All Saints," etc.) were added. The "Catechism" section also has pride of place in both hymnals as key doctrinal *loci* around the six chief parts of the Small Catechism; again, *ELHB* 1912 adds a couple of elaborations (e.g., "Confirmation," and "Marriage, Family, Children"). And finally, both collections conclude with the same basic eschatological themes of "Cross and Comfort," "Death and Burial," and "Eternity"/"Heaven."

The dissimilarities between the two hymnals have more to do with rearranging than with adding anything new to *ELHB* 1912. For instance, *ELHB* 1912 includes 130 hymns before it ever gets to "Advent" and the beginning of the Church Year (as compared to only 14 hymns in *ELHB* 1892). Yet, almost all of the preliminary headings prior to "Advent" in *ELHB* 1912 were already found elsewhere in *ELHB* 1892. Another significant change is the renaming of the section "The Word and the Church" in *ELHB* 1892 to simply "Church" in *ELHB* 1912. In *ELHB* 1892, this section precedes the section on "Catechism"; in *ELHB* 1912, it follows it. Finally, the section on "The Christian Life" in *ELHB* 1892 is renamed as "Sanctification" in *ELHB* 1912 and significantly reshaped in the titles of its subcategories.

Taking a look at the larger picture, when one compares the outlines of thematic headings between *KELG* 1847, *ELHB* 1889, *ELHB* 1892, and *ELHB* 1912, an overall pattern emerges. First of all, Crull's *ELHB* 1889 sought to emulate Walther's *KELG* 1847 closely in its thematic headings. (See Appendix Three.) Although the exact wording of the headings in *ELHB* 1889 is not as elaborate as *KELG* 1847, the order in which the categories appear is identical between the two. Nothing is rearranged, though some lesser categories in *KELG* 1847 are omitted from *ELHB* 1889 (e.g., "Table Hymns" and "Hymns on One's Station and Calling"). In other words, Crull's *ELHB* 1889 is clearly intended to be ordered according to Walther's outline in *KELG* 1847.

The addition of sub-categories in *ELHB* 1892 suggests a pragmatic elaboration of the bare-bones outline provided in *ELHB* 1889. The elaborations are pragmatic in that they provided a kind of index for the pastor to find hymns by specific topic. With the addition of fifty new hymns at the back of *ELHB* 1892, this became even more critical, since these hymns were also, within their own section (titled "Additional Hymns"), ordered according to the outline for the rest of the hymnal. Thus, for example, with the *ELHB* 1892 addition of the sub-category of "Prayer" under the heading "Catechism," the user could easily see that hymns 176 ("Our Father, Thou in Heaven Above") and 413 ("Our Heavenly Father, Hear") would both pertain. (See Figure 16.) More than pragmatic, however, this feature also reflects a pastoral and doctrinal concern articulated by Walther, that with a hymnal containing a flood of so many new hymns, one needed to become familiar with where the principal hymns on a given doctrine were located.

The advent of *ELHB* 1912, however, signaled a shift in approach. Beginning already with the proposed headings in the 1905 *Lutheran Witness* article, the move toward *ELHB* 1912 brought with it a greater flexibility in how the hymns in the hymnal were organized. The editors felt free to modify and adapt the tradition they had received from *KELG* 1847. Although they were careful not to drop any of the main categories from *ELHB* 1892, they did rearrange and occasionally modify the titles of some of the categories. The following summary shows the big-picture changes in hymn organization between *KELG* 1847 and *ELHB* 1912:

KELG 1847	*ELHB* 1912
Opening/Closing	Opening/Closing
	Praise and Worship Themes
Church Year	Church Year
Word and the Church	Justification & Sanctification
Catechism	Catechism
Justification & Christian Life	Church
End Times	End Times

The most significant thematic shift was the insertion of over a hundred hymns related to various aspects of praise and worship at the beginning of the hymn section, ahead of the Church Year. All of these themes were found elsewhere in *KELG* 1847 and moved to the front of *ELHB* 1912. A second major thematic shift is the exchanging of places between "Justification and Sanctification/Christian Life" and "Word/Church" sections. Since no minutes or records have survived from the *ELHB* 1912 committee, it is impossible to know precisely the reasons for these changes. Whatever the case, the changes in hymn heading organization do reflect a willingness on the part of the editors of *ELHB* 1912 to adapt and rearrange the categories received from Walther's *KELG* 1847.

The Sluggish Arrival of ELHB 1912

With the outline and hymns proposed and adopted at the 1905 Convention, it seemed that the publication of a revision of *ELHB* 1892 would be imminent. However, at the 1907 Convention the Hymn Book Committee reported:

> According to the proceedings of the last session of Synod, p. 67, Synod resolved "That the committee go ahead with publishing the hymn book only under the condition that it place no financial burden upon Synod."
>
> The committee found no ways and means of publishing the book without placing any financial burden on Synod, and the book was not published. But your committee used the time to make improvements on the hymnal. The musical setting of the common service was published, also the morning, evening and communion service in separate form for congregational use.
>
> Your committee now requests the Synod to instruct the Publication Board to publish the work in conjunction with the hymn book committee, removing the restriction imposed by Synod on your committee at the last session . . .[104]

Synod adopted the committee's report, and "voted to remove the restrictions of [the] last convention in regard to the publishing of the new hymn-book . . ."[105] Yet, by the 1909 Convention, the committee was still hindered in bringing the revision to publication, reporting "that the new hymn-book with tunes was not published, because they [the committee] had not been able to secure the necessary funds for this purpose."[106]

---

[104] "Proceedings of the Tenth Convention of the Evangelical Lutheran Synod of Missouri and Other States," in Milwaukee, 1907 (Pittsburgh: American Lutheran Publication Board), 66.

[105] Ibid., 64.

[106] "Proceedings of the Eleventh Convention of the Evangelical Lutheran Synod of Missouri and Other States," in Cleveland, 1909 (Pittsburgh: American Lutheran Publication Board), 79.

A widespread frustration with delays was apparent in a March 1908 report from the American Lutheran Publication Board, the publishing arm of the English Synod.

> The appearance of the Church Hymnal is still the subject of inquiry, wonder, and perhaps anxiety, among us. The correspondence incumbent upon the Publication Board throughout the years that this publication has been the object of hope, has very probably entailed an amount of labor equivalent to the amount necessary to produce the book. As it is, the manuscript is still in the hands of the committee entrusted with the work of its preparation and this Board is still faithfully engaged in the attempt of quieting impatient enquirers and of appeasing its own resentment in case it is blamed for the delay.[107]

The article continues by noting the additional problem for the Publication Board of living in a state of limbo between hymnals. Because the new hymnal appeared to be on the horizon, demand for the old hymnal was decreasing, as many congregations preferred to wait for the new edition. "How much the sale of our present book has been hindered by the protracted expectation of the new book, is not readily appreciated."[108]

And yet, sales of *ELHB* 1889/1892 appear to have been steady and healthy, over all. Theodore J. A. Huegli (1861–1933), who had earlier prepared an index of the official Proceedings of the English Synod from 1888–1907,[109] wrote a follow up series of articles in the *Lutheran Witness* titled "The History of Synod." Perhaps in response to the somewhat negative report of the Publication Board a month earlier, Huegli took up the topic of "The Hymn Book" in April 1908, outlining a history of *ELHB* 1889/1892 and its various editions according to the proceedings he had recently indexed. Toward the conclusion of his article, he notes: "So then we have now four kinds of Hymnals. 1. The

---

[107] "Report of the American Lutheran Publication Board," *Lutheran Witness* 27, no. 6 (1908), 43.

[108] Ibid.

[109] This index was published in the back of "Proceedings of the Tenth Convention of the Evangelical Lutheran Synod of Missouri and Other States," 90–112.

unabridged.[110] 2. The abridged.[111] 3. The Hymn Pamphlet.[112] 4. One hundred hymns with music."[113] He continues: "The Hymnbook was seemingly a good seller. Let us see."

It was copyrighted in 1892. Seven years later [1899] the report says: "The Hymn Book experiences a regular sale." Nine years later [1901] the report says: "The Hymn Book has been repeatedly issued in increased editions, due largely to the in-

---

[110] *Evangelical Lutheran Hymn Book*, (Baltimore: Lutheran Publication Board, 1892). This edition appears to be the most complete edition published prior to *ELHB* 1912. It contained the Common Service materials of 1888 (first added in this edition), including tables for: the festivals of the Church Year, the Epistles and Gospels, Scripture lessons for Sundays and festivals, and daily readings for morning and evening; orders of service for Holy Communion, Vespers, and Matins; Introits and Collects for the Church Year; Invitatories, Antiphons, Responsories and Versicles for the Church Year; a section of collects and prayers, as well as longer corporate prayers such as the Litany, Suffrages, and the Bidding Prayer; the Psalms (selected); 450 hymns; and indexes.

[111] *Evangelical Lutheran Hymn Book*, abbreviated ed. (Pittsburgh: American Lutheran Publication Board, 1905). According to the "Catalogue of the American Lutheran Publication Board," printed at the back of "Proceedings of the Ninth Convention of the Evangelical Lutheran Synod of Missouri and Other States," this edition appears to have been first published in 1905. It contained only the Order of Morning and Evening Service and 450 hymns. The catalogue notes that: "This cheap and abbreviated edition may prove very useful to the needs of poor mission churches."

[112] These inexpensive offprints of various hymns in *ELHB* 1892 appear to have been first published around 1899. The "Catalogue of the American Lutheran Publication Board," printed at the back of "Proceedings of the Ninth Convention of the Evangelical Lutheran Synod of Missouri and Other States," describes three different types of "Hymn Pamphlets" published by 1905: "Hymn Booklet" (35 hymns, morning and evening services, "For Mission Congregations and Travelling Missionaries"); "Passion Hymns" (ten hymns); and "Hymn Sheet" (nine hymns, "suitable for Mission Festivals, Dedication, Cornerstone Laying, Reformation Festivals, Installation, and similar occasions."

[113] *One Hundred Hymns with Music: For Mission Congregations and Sunday Schools*, (Pittsburgh: American Lutheran Publication Board, 1901). This edition appears to have been first published around 1901 as an inexpensive offprint of selected hymns from *ELHB* 1892.

troductory rate that was granted." Two years later [1903] the report says: "New Editions, Hymn Book, 11,200 copies," and "Hymn Pamphlet 5,000 copies." One year later [1905] the report says: "New Edition Hymn Book 11,000 copies, including 5,000 of the abbreviated ones, and "Hymn Pamphlet 5,000 copies." Two years later [1907] the report says: "New Edition Full Hymnal 8,000 copies. Abridged Hymnal 4,000 copies. One Hundred Hymns with music 10,000 copies."[114]

Although records of the various printings of *ELHB* from 1889 onward are incomplete in the English Synod's Proceedings, a conservative estimate would suggests that at least 60,000 copies of the "abridged" and "unabridged" versions of *ELHB* were printed over the two decades between 1889 and 1909.

At the 1909 Convention, the Hymn Book Committee once again reported that "the new hymn-book with tunes was not published, because they had not been able to secure the necessary funds for this purpose." Synod then appointed a committee of three laymen to secure funds for publishing the new hymnal.[115]

The question of hymnal publication at the 1909 Convention, however, took a backseat to the much larger issue of the so-called "Union Question"—that is, whether and how the English Synod might join the German Missouri Synod as the English District. German Missouri had appointed a committee to meet with representatives of the English Synod on the day prior to the opening of the 1909 Convention. Together they agreed on a report that was presented to the convention for consideration. There were seven points that the convention adopted, the very first of which was:

> 1. That we turn our publication affairs over to the German Synod, but that a committee, the majority of which are members of the English district, be elected to get out such literature as our peculiar needs demand such as the Hymnbook, Sunday-school literature, Pamphlets, etc.[116]

---

[114] Theodore J. A. Huegli, "The History of Synod: The Hymn Book," *Lutheran Witness* 27, no. 7 (1908), 54.

[115] "Proceedings of the Eleventh Convention of the Evangelical Lutheran Synod of Missouri and Other States," 79.

[116] [Carl A.] W.[eiss], "Convention of Synod," *Lutheran Witness* 28, no. 15

Following the 1909 Convention, the Hymn Book Committee continued its work on preparing a manuscript for publication. In February 1910, the Publication Board reported:

> Efforts are being made by a Committee appointed for the purpose and by the President and Officers of Synod to place the new Hymnal with music into the hands of our people. We have good reason to hope that any further delay will be shortly overcome . . .[117]

In December of the same year, a notice in the *Lutheran Witness* reported of the new hymnal: "The plates are now being made. The printer promises three or four pages every day."[118]

Problems with the printer appear to have plagued the project from here on out. In March 1911, the Publication Board reported:

> The New Hymn book is being published in both a Music and a Word edition[.] With reference to the repeated change in date set for its prospective appearance, which has been a source of disappointment to many, we wish to have the brethren bear in mind that the Board has been entirely dependent for information of this kind on advices [sic] received from the printer.[119]

Two months later, at the final convention of the English Synod, the report from the March *Lutheran Witness* was included in the Pro-

---

(1909), 323.

[117] William H. Dale, "Report of the American Lutheran Publication Board," *Lutheran Witness* 29, no. 4 (1910): 30.

[118] "Coming," *Lutheran Witness* 29, no. 25 (1910): 200. It appears that Dallmann secured the printer for *ELHB* 1912, as he notes in his autobiography: "I was chairman of the Hymnal Committee from the beginning, and now the tune edition was gracefully placed into my lap for publication. No music printer in Milwaukee! I found a taverner who had set music years ago. A handful of music type was bought, and he set up a few pages during the day and sent them to me. I alone had to read proof in a hurry and rush it back the same night so that he could distribute the type and set up a few more pages the next day—and so to the weary end! Then the work was presented to Concordia Publishing House . . ." Dallmann, *My Life,* 107.

[119] William H. Dale, "Publication Matters: Report of American Lutheran Publication Board," *Lutheran Witness* 30, no. 7 (1911): 52.

ceedings.[120] At the convention of the German Missouri Synod, each of the proposed seven points of union were considered separately, to which the German convention then added their own clarifications as to how they understood each of the seven points. Regarding the first point having to do with publications, the German Synod added the following clarification:

> 1. The publications in question are subject to revision by the Theological Faculty at St. Louis, and the English District is to assume the financial responsibility for such publications in the same manner as is now done in similar instances by our German Districts.

In effect, it appears that the German Synod desired to exercise doctrinal oversight over future English District publications, but not to invest any of its financial resources toward their publication. Yet, in the English Synod's consideration of the German Synod's clarification, it was resolved that President Eckhardt of the English Synod be added to the Preliminary Committee,[121] and that this committee be empowered "to act in all matters to be adjusted between our District Synod and the Delegate Synod."[122] It was also resolved that ". . . the Hymn-Book Committee, the Hymn-Book Finance Committee, were continued until they have wound up their affairs."[123]

The publication of the new hymnal would take nearly another year

---

[120] "Proceedings of the Twelfth Convention of the Evangelical Lutheran Synod of Missouri and Other States," 66.

[121] The Preliminary Committee had been appointed at the 1909 Convention to work out matters of the union with the German Missouri Synod. See "Proceedings of the Eleventh Convention of the Evangelical Lutheran Synod of Missouri and Other States," 47. That committee was authorized to continue its work following the 1911 union. See "Proceedings of the Twelfth Convention of the Evangelical Lutheran Synod of Missouri and Other States," 45: *Executive Preliminary Committee*, authorized to adjust matters with German Synod of Missouri, Ohio, and Other States, and to make necessary transfers of properties, etc.: Rev. H. P. Eckhardt; Prof. Geo. Romoser; Rev. W. Dallmann; Messrs. J. M. Schuermann, E. Stuerken."

[122] "Proceedings of the Twelfth Convention of the Evangelical Lutheran Synod of Missouri and Other States," 72.

[123] Ibid., 46.

to materialize. By February 1912, it appears that the project had already been put into the hands of Concordia Publishing House for publication. A notice from the publisher appeared in the *Lutheran Witness* expressing regret that a precise publication date could not yet be announced. This was due mainly to the contract that the American Lutheran Publication Board had previously made with the printer, which left Concordia "without effective means to force more rapid progress." And yet, more than half of the hymnal was now printed, and Concordia hoped to see the complete book (with tunes) available for distribution sometime in the early spring. Yet, "This announcement," Concordia concluded, "is no promise on our part. We cannot make promises in this matter because our frequent disappointments in this deal have taught us the folly of essaying a promise without having reasonable control over the conditions attending the execution of such promise."[124]

Finally, in April 1912, Concordia Publishing House was pleased to announce in the *Lutheran Witness* "the completion of the new hymnal [tune edition only], which has so long and so eagerly been expected." Those who had placed advanced orders with the English District at a special price would receive their copies first. A second printing would commence as soon as the plates arrived at Concordia.[125] The word edition was not yet ready, though the plates were in process.[126]

---

[124] "The New English Hymnal," *Lutheran Witness* 31, no. 5 (1912): 40.

[125] "Our New English Hymn-Book," *Theological Quarterly* 16, no. 3 (1912): 155, notes that: "At its final convention in St. Louis the Synod's Hymn-Book Committee reported that it had finished its work, and 'that the Hymnal is in the hands of the printer.' With this committee another, the Hymn-Book Finance Committee, had been cooperating, and this committee reported that it had received 4,802 advance subscriptions for the new hymnal—enough to almost exhaust the first edition; that it had received $3,224.65, had expended $1,821.50, had outstanding accounts for unpaid subscriptions to the amount of $728.75—all of which showed that the financial side of the enterprise had been sufficiently safe-guarded." By July 1912, the publisher announced that the first printing had sold out. See "At Home," *Lutheran Witness* 31, no. 14 (1912): 109. Nearly two months later, the publisher announced that the second printing had arrived and was now available for purchase. See "The New Hymn-Book," *Lutheran Witness* 31, no. 18 (1912): 144.

[126] "The Evangelical Lutheran Hymn-Book," *Lutheran Witness* 31, no. 10 (1912): 72. The production of the word edition appears to have been a

Three weeks later, the *Lutheran Witness* published a review of the *Evangelical Lutheran Hymnal* [sic], which consisted mostly of excerpts from correspondence received from the publisher:

> At last we are able to announce the completion of this book which has been so long in preparation, long in the hands of the editorial committee, which has exercised the most scrupulous care in the selection of text and melody; long in the hands of the committee of revision; long in the hands of the executive committee and—be it confessed—long in the hands of the printers. It is sincerely hoped by the publishers that all this painstaking care will have resulted in giving the Missouri-Lutheran congregations a hymnal that shall be not only orthodox to a nicety, but also both comprehensive as to text selection and complete and practical as to its musical settings.[127]

Understandably, the publisher clearly wanted to distance itself from the delay experienced as a result of committees and, in particular, the printer.

Two brief reviews appeared in the publications of German Missouri to announce the advent of the tune edition of *ELHB* 1912. *Lehre und Wehre* noted that the collection should be welcomed with joy not only by organists, but also by families in their homes, with the hope that its hymns might displace some of the songs that are unworthy to be sung by Christian families.[128] *Der Lutheraner* provided a glowing

---

Concordia Publishing House project. It was not available for sale until December 1912. See [George A.] R[omoser], "Review of *Evangelical Lutheran Hymn-Book,* Word Edition," *Lutheran Witness* 32, no. 2 (1913): 15.

[127] [George A.] R[omoser], "Review of *Evangelical Lutheran Hymnal* [sic]," *Lutheran Witness* 31, no. 10 (1912): 80.

[128] F.[riedrich] B.[ente], "Review of *Evangelical Lutheran Hymn-Book, With Tunes,*" *Lehre und Wehre* 58, no. 5 (1912): 218: "Unser Englischer Distrikt kann sich glücklich schätzen, daß er in den Besitz dieses Buches gelangt ist, welches Kirchenlieder und Melodien miteinander verbindet. Nicht bloß Organisten werden es mit Freuden begrüßen, sondern auch in christliche Familien sollte es seinen Eingang halten und mit dazu beitragen, daß unsere Kirchenlieder nicht nur in den Gottesdiensten, sondern auch in den Häusern fleißig gesungen und unwürdige Lieder aus christlichen Familien verdrängt werden. Wer eine Orgel oder eine Piano im Hause hat, sollte sich unverzüglich dies Hymn-Book with Tunes kommen

description of the contents of *ELHB* 1912, noting that a large part of the hymns included were "translations of our old German Lutheran hymns," that the remainder of the hymns were "chosen with care," and that the hymns were arranged according to the Church Year, chief doctrinal *loci,* and various occasions.[129]

The most thorough and substantive review of *ELHB* 1912 appeared in the October 1912 issue of *Theological Quarterly.* The unnamed writer begins:

> While the English Synod of Missouri was discussing the advisability and feasibility of organic union with the German Missouri Synod, a great work was quietly being done for it which was destined to affect, in a perceptible manner, the public worship and private devotions of its members. At its final convention in St. Louis the Synod's Hymn-Book Committee reported that it had finished its work, and 'that the Hymnal is in the hands of the printer.' . . . In the mean time [sic], the contemplated union with the German Synod was effected . . . The new hymnal therefore, by the logic of events becomes the hymnal of the entire Missouri Synod.[130]

The reviewer continues by first noting the magnitude of change from *ELHB* 1892 to *ELHB* 1912. He calculates that *ELHB* 1912 contains an additional 135 new hymns, and then provides lists of first the

---

lassen. Und Pastoren tun insonderheit englischen Gemeindegliedern einen Dienst, wenn sie dieselben auf obiges Buch aufmerksam machen."

[129] E.[dward] P.[ardieck], "Review of *Evangelical Lutheran Hymn-Book*," *Der Lutheraner* 68, no. 10 (1912): 159: "Ein schöner, stattlicher Band von 538 Seiten, das Gesangbuch für unsere englischen Gemeinden, an das ein Komitee unserer englischen Brüder viel Arbeit und Mühe gewandt hat. Es enthält eine volle Gottesdienstordnung für den Hauptgottesdienst, für Abend- und Frühgottesdienst, Antiphonen, Kollekten und Gebete und eine große Auswahl von Psalmen. Dann folgen die 594 Lieder mit Noten, zum sehr großen Teil Übersetzungen unserer alten deutschen lutherischen Lieder. Die übrigen sind mit Vorsicht ausgewählt. Die Lieder sind geordnet nach den Zeiten des Kirchenjahres, nach Hauptstücken der Lehre und nach Gelegenheiten. Den Schluß bilden Angaben der beweglichen und unbeweglichen Feste, die Daten des Osterfestes bis zum Jahre 2000 und mehrere Verzeichnisse."

[130] "Our New English Hymn-Book," 155.

English-language hymns that were omitted, and then the German-language hymns. And yet, he notes the "ample compensation provided" by the inclusion of additional translations of German hymns, remarking in particular that the fine translation of Speratus' "Es ist das Heil uns kommen her" "balances the loss of many of the discarded hymns." The writer estimates that "the new hymn-book contains 219 translations of standard German hymns, to 210 translations contained in the old book. About 39 percent of the entire contents of the new book is from standard Lutheran hymn-writers."[131]

The writer then reckons that the most striking change from "old to new" appears in the topical rearrangement of the hymns. "Here a veritable revolution has taken place . . . Everything appears differently grouped and differently placed." The writer suggests that

> . . . when all this is considered, one anticipates a shock among the users of the old book when they begin to use the new. It was a heroic committee that attempted this thoroughgoing change; and the question can only be, Was the committee's courage balanced by wisdom?[132]

The writer observes that this massive change runs along two lines. First, a great many hymns that appeared under one heading in *ELHB* 1892 were reclassified and now appear under a different heading in *ELHB* 1912. For some hymns, this has actually been a helpful move. Secondly, however, the writer notes that "the sequence of the topical divisions has been changed . . ." The logic of the new arrangement is apparent to the writer, in that "it follows a natural line of thought, and thus will facilitate our mental readjustment of the new order of things."[133] The writer finishes his review by noting a number of additional positive features of *ELHB* 1912 and concludes that "in our judgment the book will help to make our English services more beautiful, more impressive, and more expressive of the Lutheran ideal of divine worship . . ."[134]

---

[131] Ibid., 157–58.
[132] Ibid., 159.
[133] Ibid., 160–61.
[134] Ibid., 162.

Conclusion

The trajectory from *KELG* 1847 to *ELHB* 1889/1892 to *ELHB* 1912 demonstrates both a strong continuity with Missouri's German hymnic tradition as well as a willingness to adapt the received tradition in a way that would best serve their future in an increasingly English-speaking, American context.

Walther's *KELG* 1847 represented a repudiation of the Rationalist hymnals of his day and a restoration of the older, orthodox Dresden line of hymnals. Crull sought to carry forward the substance of Walther's restorational move, both in the transitional hymnals he edited, as well as in the German hymn corpus and outline of hymns in *ELHB* 1889. Virtually all of the German hymns in *ELHB* 1889 came from *KELG* 1847; the structural outline of hymns in *ELHB* 1889 heavily mirrored *KELG* 1847. Crull had grown up in Walther's congregation and later became Walther's "go-to guy" for hymn translations and translations into English in general. Clearly, Crull's singular vision and editorship of *ELHB* 1889 was firmly grounded in Missouri's German hymnic tradition.

And yet, when it came to selecting a corpus of English-language hymns for *ELHB* 1889, Crull turned to the hymnals of older, non-Synodical Conference Lutheran church bodies (i.e., the General Synod and the General Council), with whom Missouri had been engaged in polemical discourse for decades. Indeed, the theological tensions between the more Americanized Lutherans and the Missouri Synod appear to have taken a back seat when English-speaking Missourians began to search for a roadmap to English-language hymnody. They found that roadmap by culling through the hymnals of these older Lutheran church bodies who generations earlier had already travelled the road from German into English hymnody.

Crull sought to bring the two worlds together in *ELHB* 1889—German and English hymnody, on a nearly perfect, fifty-fifty basis. Yet, almost immediately upon completion of his manuscript, Crull's single-minded vision was compromised (at least from his perspective), as a new committee quickly added an additional fifty hymns, and as the English Synod began almost immediately the long and tortuous journey toward a tune book and the eventual wholesale revision that resulted in *ELHB* 1912.

The twenty-year journey to *ELHB* 1912 was fraught with challenges, and yet this lengthy period also allowed those who worked on this project significant opportunity for reflection. Unlike *ELHB* 1889, which was almost entirely the work of one individual and a small committee of reviewers, the committee that produced *ELHB* 1912 benefitted from the requested input of any and all interested parties in the English Synod, as well as from many years of using *ELHB* 1889/1892 and learning from its plusses and minuses. Such a broadened base of input as well as significant time to reflect figured significantly into the work of the *ELHB* 1912 committee and the decisions that it made.

In their restructuring of the hymns, the *ELHB* 1912 committee retained virtually all of the chief categories from *ELHB* 1892, but with significant adaptations in the ordering of these categories. On the one hand, this shift in structure represented a "veritable revolution" to the end-user who was used to the way the hymns had been organized in *ELHB* 1892, and even *KELG* 1847. On the other hand, such a flexibility in rethinking old categories in new ways also represented a forward-thinking willingness to adapt this structural component of Missouri's German tradition in a way that would best serve in a twentieth-century, English-speaking, American context.

The legacy of Crull's work as hymnal editor and translator has been widely felt in American Lutheranism for well over a century—particularly in the Missouri Synod and other Lutheran church bodies associated with the Synodical Conference. We can attribute in no small part the Missouri Synod's ongoing and widespread use of German Lutheran hymnody from the sixteenth and seventeenth centuries to August Crull and his commitment to preserving and transitioning this great body of the church's song into Missouri's English-speaking future. The same can also be said of Crull's critical discernment of English-language hymnody in ecumenical use during his day, opening up a new world of hymnological treasures to Missouri Synod Lutherans. As an English Synod writer from this period would write (citing Luther, Watts, and Wesley—all in one sentence):

> God's praise is worthy of man's most perfect literary expression; and when Isaac Watts and Martin Luther and Wesley wrote the most beautiful hymns in the world they brought to the task all their literary skill and ability, their sentiment is lofty and inspiring, the music noble and uplifting.[135]

---

[135] "Editorial," *Lutheran Witness* 20, no. 5 (1901): 34.

APPENDIX ONE

German-Language Hymns from Pre-ELHB 1889 Collections

English Title	German Title	KELG 1847	DH 1879	LH 1882	HELC 1886	ELHB 1889
A Healer t' Us Is Given	Ein Artz ist uns gegeben	—		18		—
A Mighty Fortress Is Our God	Ein 'feste Burg ist unser Gott	158	45	7	17	135
Abide, O Dearest Jesus	Ach bleib mit deiner Gnade	2	6		2	2
All Glory Be to God on High	Allein Gott in der Höh' sei Ehr	1	1	1	1	1
Awake, My Heart, with Gladness	Auf, auf, mein Herz, mit Freuden	97	29			88
Baptized into Thy Name Most Holy	Ich bin getauft auf deinen Namen	458	59			177
Blessed Jesus, at Thy Word	Liebster Jesu, wir sind hier	8	3	3	4	4
Blessed Jesus, Here We Stand	Liebster Jesu, hier sind wir	190	58		22	178
Bless Our Going Out, O Lord	Unsern Ausgang segne Gott	—		17		—
Christ, Thou the Champion of the Band Who Own	Christe, du Beistand deiner Kreuzgemeine	167	49			141
Come, Holy Spirit, God and Lord	Komm, heiliger Geist, Herre Gott	134	38		14	111
Commit Thou All Thy Griefs	Befiehl du deine Wege	355	107			339
Dear Christians, One and All Rejoice	Nun freut euch, lieben Christen g'mein	243	68	10	25	209
Deck Thyself, My Soul, with Gladness	Schmücke dich, o liebe Seele	210	61			182
Draw us to Thee, for Then Shall We*	Zeuch uns nach dir	124	36			100
Farewell! I Say with Gladness*	Valet will ich dir geben	426	116			371
Fear Not, O Little Flock, the Foe	Verzage nicht, du Häuflein klein	455	47			143
For Me to Live Is Jesus	Christus, der ist mein Leben	400	112	15	30	372
From Heaven above to Earth I Come	Vom Himmel hoch	41	14		9	22

72 | August Crull and the Story of *ELHB* 1912

God Who Madest Earth and Heaven	Gott des Himmels und der Erden	297	84			287
I Fall Asleep in Jesus' Wounds	In Christi Wunden schlaf' ich ein	412	113	16	31	375
If Thou but Suffer God to Guide Thee	Wer nur den lieben Gott lässt walten	382	104			350
In Death's Strong Grasp the Saviour Lay	Christ lag in Todes Banden	99	28			93
In God, My Faithful God	Auf meinen lieben Gott	354	103			351
In Grateful Songs Your Voices Raise	Nun danket all und bringet Ehr	347	96			—
In Peace and Joy I Now Depart	Mit Fried' und Freud'	65	111			54
Jerusalem, Thou City Fair and High	Jerusalem, du hochgebaute Stadt	443	130		33	393
Jesus Christ, My Sure Defense	Jesus, meine Zuversicht	111	30		12	94
Jesus Christ, Our Blessed Savior	Jesus Christus, unser Heiland	110	60	14	23	183
Jesus Sinners Doth Receive	Jesus nimmt die Sünder an	222	65		24	195
Jesus, Grant that Balm and Healing*	Jesu, deine heil'gen Wunden	77	22			69
Jesus, Jesus, Jesus Only*	Jesus, Jesus, nichts als Jesus	253	74			230
Jesus, Priceless Treasure	Jesu, meine Freude	251	75			232
Jesus, Thy Blood and Righteousness	Christi Blut und Gerechtigkeit	—	70			213
Let Me Be Thine Forever	Lass mich dein sein und bleiben	174	50	6	20	156
Let Us All with Gladsome Voice	Lasst uns alle fröhlich sein	28	13		8	29
Lift Up Your Heads, Ye Mighty Gates	Macht hoch die Tür	31				30
Lord Grant That E'er We Pure Retain*	Herr Gott, erhalt uns für und für	179	53			171
Lord Jesus Christ, in Thee Alone	Allein zu dir, Herr Jesu Christ	213	64			196
Lord Jesus Christ, dich zu uns wend	Herr Jesu Christ, dich zu uns wend	4	2	2	3	6
Lord Jesus Christ, to Us Attend*	Herr Jesu Christ, dich zu uns wend	165	48	4	19	158
Lord Jesus Christ, with Us Abide	Ach, bleib bei uns, Herr Jesu Christ	270			27	256
Lord, as Thou Wilt, Deal Thou with Me	Herr, wie du willst, so schick's mit mir					
Lord, Keep Us in Thy Word and Work	Erhalt uns, Herr	159	46		18	138
Lord, to Thee I Make Confession	Herr, ich habe missgehandelt	—	66			—

English Title	German Title	KELG 1847	DH 1879	LH 1882	HELC 1886	ELHB 1889
My Soul, Now Bless Thy Maker	Nun lob', mein' Seel', den Herren	348	97			319
Now Do We Pray God, the Holy Ghost*	Nun bitten wir den heiligen Geist	136	39			120
Now God Be with Us, for the Night Is Closing	Die Nacht ist kommen	314	89			300
Now I Have Found the Sure Foundation	Ich habe nun den Grund gefunden	240	69	11	26	217
Now Lay We Calmly in the Grave	Nun lasst uns den Leib begraben	417	119		32	380
Now Let Us Come before Him*	Nun lasst uns gehn und treten	54	17			44
Now Rest beneath Night's Shadows	Nun ruhen alle Wälder	319	88			301
Now Thank We All Our God	Nun danket alle Gott	346	95	13	5	321
O Bleeding Head, and Wounded	O Haupt voll Blut und Wunden	84	21		11	74
O Christ, Our True and Only Light	O Jesu Christe, wahres Licht	175	51	5	21	162
O Darkest Woe	O Traurigkeit, o Herzeleid	88	26			75
O God, Thou Faithful God	O Gott, du frommer Gott	281	79	12	28	265
O Holy Spirit, Enter in	O heil'ger Geist, kehr' bei uns ein	140	40			119
O How Blest Are Ye Whose Toils Are Ended*	O wie selig seid ihr doch, ihr Frommen	424	120			381
O Lamb of God, Most Holy	O Lamm Gottes, unschuldig	86	19			76
O Lord Our Father, Thanks to Thee	Herr Gott Vater, wir preisen dich	51	16			45
O Lord, How Shall I Meet Thee	Wie soll ich dich empfangen	44	12		7	32
O Lord, I Love Thee from My Heart*	Herzlich lieb hab' ich dich, o Herr	271	80			266
O Lord, My God, I Cry to Thee	O Herre Gott, in meiner Not	420	114			382
O Morning Star! How Fair and Bright	Wie schön leuchet der Morgenstern	261	76			239
Our Father, Thou in Heaven Above	Vater unser im Himmelreich	185	57			176
Out of the Depths I Cry to Thee	Aus tiefer Not schrei ich zu dir	214	63	9		200
Praise to the Lord, the Almighty, the King	Lobe den Herren, den mächtigen König der Ehren	341	93			326

Since Christ Has Gone to Heaven, His Home	Auf Christi Himmelfahrt allein	117	35		13	105
Tender Shepherd, Thou Hast Stilled	Guter Hirt, du hast gestillt	—	124			—
That Man a Godly Life Might Live	Dies sind die heil'gen zehn Gebot	180	55			172
The Lord My God Be Praised*	Gelobet sei der Herr	21	43			128
The Old Year Now Hath Passed Away	Das alte Jahr vergangen ist	48	42		10	47
Thou Who Art Three in Unity	Der du bist drei in Einigkeit	143	42		15	131
To God, the Father of All Love*	Sei Lob und Her' dem höchsten Gut	350	94		6	332
Wake, Awake, for Night Is Flying	Wachet auf! ruft uns die Stimme	436	125			399
We All Believe in One True God, Maker	Wir glauben all' an einen Gott, Schöpfer	183	56	8	16	175
Whatever God Ordains Is Good*	Was Gott thut, das ist wohlgethan	376	106		29	363
When in the Hour of Utmost Need	Wenn wir in höchsten Nöten sein	387	102			364
When My Last Hour Is Close at Hand	Wenn mein Stündlein vorhanden ist	428	115			385
Who Knows How Near My End May Be	Wer weiss, wie nahe mir mein Ende	429	117			386

*Indicates that the hymn is found by a different English title in one of the predecessor collections.

None of the hymns from the appendix in KELG 1856 were included in the English-language volumes.

English titles are as they appear in ELHB 1889.

80 hymns total.

APPENDIX TWO

English-Language Hymns from Non-Missouri Synod Hymnals

Hymn Title	ELHB 1889	DH 1879	CB 1868	BoW 1870	ELH 1880
Hymns from 4 of 4 Hymnals (25)					
Abide with me! fast falls the eventide	368	90	59	532	440
Alas! and did my Saviour bleed	59	23	181	128	64
Almighty God, Thy Word is cast	3	8	56	592	10
Asleep in Jesus! blessed sleep	370	122	555	560	443
Awake, my soul, and with the sun	286	85	510	515	301
Before Jehovah's awful throne	311	98	1	1	157
Come hither, ye faithful, triumphantly sing	20	15	129	233	38
From Greenland's icy mountains	144	52	297	221	163
God moves in a mysterious way	344	108	82	76	175
Great God, we sing that mighty Hand	42	18	137	545	50
Hail to the Lord's Anointed	23	11	122	153	22
Hail, Thou once despised Jesus	67	25	170	150	90
Jerusalem, my happy home	391	129	579	590	466
Jesus, the very thought of Thee	233	73	224	176	284
Just as I am, without one plea	214	72	366	311	241
Lord, dismiss us with Thy blessing	5	9	58	594	12
My soul, repeat His praise	320	99	74	3	367
O God of Jacob, by whose hand	264	81	91	86	331
O Thou, from whom all goodness flows	358	109	490	378	426

76 | August Crull and the Story of *ELHB* 1912

Our Lord is risen from the dead	104	37	199	245	95
Rock of Ages, cleft for me	220	71	367	310	255
Saviour, when in dust to Thee	78	67	172	137	242
That day of wrath, that dreadful day	395	127	566	567	459
The Lord my pasture shall prepare	241	77	85	73	173
When all Thy mercies, O my God	334	100	17	75	369

Hymns from 3 of 4 Hymnals (52)

Am I a soldier of the Cross?	244		461	456	382
And must this body die	369		561	476	450
Christ the Lord is risen to-day	90	31	192	239	
Christ whose glory fills the skies	224	86	40	516	109
Come, Holy Spirit, come	110		254	324	
Come, Holy Spirit, heavenly Dove	112	41	253	182	
Come, said Jesus' sacred voice	191		347	279	375
Come, to Calvary's holy mountain	64		349	273	379
Day of wrath! that day of mourning	388	128	569		460
Father of glory, to Thy name	125		125	65	117
Father of heaven, whose love profound	126		263	63	114
Father, in whom we live	124		261	64	118
For Thy mercy and Thy grace	41		138	543	41
Glorious things of thee are spoken	145		266	193	191
Go to dark Gethsemane	66		173	120	384
God is love, His mercy brightens	342		78	62	171
Grace! 'tis a charming sound	210		102	94	370
Gracious Spirit, Dove divine	114		256	186	108
Great is the Lord our God	146		269	483	201
Hark, the glad sound, the Saviour comes	24		123	111	20

Hymn Title	ELHB 1889	DH 1879	CB 1868	BoW 1870	ELH 1880
How beauteous are their feet	148		285	198	335
I know that my Redeemer lives [Medley]	92	33	209		92
I love Thy Zion, Lord	151		275	202	194
I would not live alway, I ask not to stay	376	118	542	471	
In vain would boasting reason find	153		97	309	187
Jesus shall reign where'er the sun	154		295	213	164
Jesus, and shall it ever be	228		445	174	289
Jesus, Lover of my soul	231		321	358	290
Joy to the world, the Lord is come	27		134	110	23
Let songs of praises fill the sky	116		240	179	105
Lord, it belongs not to my care	355		492	374	403
May the grace of Christ our Saviour	9		64	598	14
Nearer, my God to Thee, Nearer to Thee! E'en tho'	357	110	536	393	253
Not all the blood of beasts	73		158	135	363
O bless the Lord, my soul	322		73	7	214
O for a faith that will not shrink	262		411	357	214
Our God, our Help in ages past	383		538	389	177
Saviour, who Thy flock art feeding	274		532	258	345
Stricken, smitten, and afflicted	81		182	132	72
Sun of my soul, Thou Saviour dear	305		523	530	314
The man is ever blest	278		375	440	386
The Saviour calls, let every ear	166		345	270	372
The Spirit in our hearts	167		346	275	380
Thee we adore, eternal Lord	329		7	33	357
There is a land of pure delight	397		574	572	453
This is the day the Lord hath made	13	5	39	39	

78 | August Crull and the Story of *ELHB* 1912

Thou art the Way, to Thee alone	242		228	106	276
Through the day Thy love hath spared us	308	91	525		318
When I survey the wondrous Cross	86	24	183	127	
When streaming from the eastern skies	294		507	513	299
While with ceaseless course the sun	49		139	544	39
Zion stands with hills surrounded	170		270	484	149

Hymns from 2 of 4 Hymnals (105)

A great and mighty wonder	16		130		35
A hymn of glory let us sing	99		201		94
All hail the power of Jesus' name	222		215	149	
All that I was, my sin, my guilt	204		105	100	
And let this feeble body fail	337		491	342	
And will the Judge descend	387			570	458
And wilt Thou pardon, Lord	188		358		239
Angels from the realms of glory	53				59
Approach, my soul, the mercy seat	205		364	234	
Arise, my soul, arise	206		211	330	
As with gladness men of old	50		140	142	
Awake, my soul, in joyful lays	310			169	59
Behold the Saviour of mankind	60		179	235	368
Behold the sure Foundation-Stone	139		264	192	
Beloved, it is well	338			443	427
Blest is the man, forever blest	207			316	257
Christ, Thou art the sure Foundation	140		292	492	
Come let us join our cheerful songs	63			160	65
Come, my soul, thy suit prepare	190		29		243
Come, Thou almighty King	123		262	66	

Hymn Title	ELHB 1889	DH 1879	CB 1868	BoW 1870	ELH 1880
Dear refuge of my weary soul	340		481	367	
Delay not, delay not, O sinner	193			290	378
Enslaved by sin and bound in chains	65			137	63
Father of mercies, in Thy Word	142		310	249	
Forever with the Lord	389		585	588	
From all that dwell below the skies	313		307	9	
Give to our God immortal praise	314		100		
Glory to Thee, My God, this night	298			519	360
God of mercy, God of grace	315			418	316
God of my life, to Thee I call	345		480	463	366
God of my life, whose gracious power	248		426	376	
Great God, what do I see and hear	390	126	565		
Guide me, O Thou great Jehovah	249		418	387	
Hail the day that sees Him rise	101		200	243	
Hark, ten thousand harps and voices	102		206	162	
Hark! a voice divides the sky	373		557	562	
Hark! the herald-angels sing	25		128	230	
Hark! what mean those holy voices	26		127	229	
Hasten, O sinner, to be wise	194			285	377
Here in Thy name, eternal Lord	147			485	133
Holy Father, Thou hast taught me	251			362	40
Holy Ghost, with light divine	115		257	187	
How precious is the Book divine	149		309	253	
How shall the young secure their hearts	150		312	252	
How sweet the name of Jesus sounds	225		221	175	
I heard the voice of Jesus say	211		106	320	

I lay my sins on Jesus	212	368	313
I was a wandering sheep	227	107	99
I'll praise my Maker whilst I've breath	316	2	17
In the Cross of Christ I glory	68	157	133
In weariness and pain	353	485	381
Jerusalem the golden	392	587	467
Jesus, Brightness of the Father	132	93	124
Jesus, my great High Priest	71	210	
Lamb of God, we fall before thee	215		144	254
Let every ear attend	155		172	184
Let thoughtless thousands choose the road	394		271	452
Lo! upon the altar lies	184	337	410	272
Lord of hosts, to Thee we raise	159	294	488	
Lord of my life! O may Thy praise	289		508	300
Lord of the worlds above	7	43	48	
Lord, in Thy kingdom there shall be	157	276		199
Lord, we confess our numerous faults	216	99	318	
May we Thy precepts, Lord fulfil	161	279		391
My faith looks up to Thee	258	435	364	
My Father, cheering name	356		445	424
My soul, be on thy guard	260	463	457	
My spirit on Thy care	261	427	365	
Now may He who from the dead	10	63	599	
Now the shades of night are gone	291		518	303
O for a thousand tongues to sing	236	217	151	
O Jesus, King most wonderful	238	225	177	
O Lord, my best desire fulfil	267	420	348	
O Spirit of the living God	164	300	190	

Hymn Title	ELHB 1889	DH 1879	CB 1868	BoW 1870	ELH 1880
O that the Lord would guide my ways	269		393	354	
O Thou that hear'st when sinners cry	199		356	301	
O Thou who wouldst not have	270		361	304	
On what has now been sown	12		57		11
Prayer is the soul's sincere desire	271			326	215
Return, O wanderer, return	201			284	376
Saviour, Breathe an evening blessing	302			520	319
Shepherd of tender youth	275		526		348
Sinners, turn; why will ye die	202			289	374
Soldiers of Christ, arise	276		462	454	
Songs of immortal praise belong	327		70		166
Songs of praise the angels sang	328		13		362
Spirit of mercy, truth and love	122			247	107
Stars of the morning, so gloriously bright	134		94		125
The abyss of many a former sin	203		359		237
The atoning work is done	106			145	98
The day is past and gone	306			522	317
The Head that once was crowned with thorns	107		205		99
The year begins with Thee	48		136	136	44
There is a fountain filled with blood	82		159	575	454
There is an hour of peaceful rest	398			521	321
Thus far the Lord has led me on	309			29	6
Thy presence, gracious Lord, afford	14			78	174
Thy Ways, O Lord, with wise design	361				358
To God be glory, peace on earth	331		8		
To our Redeemer's glorious name	84			156	66

We lift our hearts to Thee	293		512		511	
We sing the almighty power of God	333			69	167
When I can read my title clear	283		380	383	
Who is this that comes from Edom	98	32	191		
Ye servants of the Lord	285		465	449	

Hymns from 1 of 4 Hymnals (9)

Blest be Thy love, dear Lord	245			404	
Chief of sinners though I be	223			287	
God who madest earth and heaven, Darkness	299	92			
Jesus, my Truth, my Way	255		436		
My God, my Father, while I stray	259	82			
Oft in sorrow, oft in woe	359			415	
Praise, O praise our God and king	325			137	
Thine for ever! God of love	281		326		
Through all the changing scenes of life	330		86		

APPENDIX THREE

Comparison of Thematic Headings in KELG 1847 and ELHB 1889

KELG 1847
I. Sunday Hymns
II. Advent and Christmas
III. The Circumcision of Jesus and the New Year
IV. Epiphany (January 6)
V. Purification of Mary (February 2)
VI. Annunciation (March 25)
VII. Passion Hymns or Hymns on the Suffering and Death of Jesus Christ
VIII. Easter Hymns or Hymns on the Resurrection of Jesus Christ
IX. Ascension of Jesus Christ
X. Pentecost Hymns or Hymns on the Pouring Out of the Holy Spirit
XI. Hymns for Trinity Sunday or on the Holy Trinity
XII. John the Baptist (June 24)
XIII. The Visitation of Mary (July 2)
XIV. St. Michael (September 29)
XV. Reformation Day (October 31)
XVI. Commemoration of the Holy Apostles
XVII. The Word of God and the Christian Church
XVIII. Catechism Hymns
   1. The Law of God
   2. The Christian Faith
   3. The Holy Lord's Prayer

ELHB 1889
1. Sunday
2. Advent and Christmas
3. New Year
4. Epiphany
5. Presentation

6. Passion

7. Easter

8. Ascension
9. Pentecost

10. Trinity

11. Michaelmas
12. Reformation

13. The Word and the Church
14. Catechism

4. Holy Baptism
5. Holy Absolution
6. The Holy Lord's Supper
XIX. Repentance and Confession
XX. Faith and Justification
XXI. Jesus Hymns
XXII. On the Christian Life
XXIII. Morning Hymns
XXIV. Table Hymns
　1. Before Meals
　2. After Meals
XXV. Evening Hymns
XXVI. Hymns on One's Station and Calling
　1. Matrimony
　2. Travel
　3. Harvest
　4. Appendix for Children
XXVII. Praise and Thanks
XXVIII. Cross and Comfort
XXIX. In Particular Times of Need
　1. General Times of Need
　2. War Time
　3. Persecution
　4. Bad Weather
　5. Great Drought
XXX. Death and Burial
XXXI. Hymns of Eternity and Hymns on the Resurrection and the Last Judgment

15. Repentance
16. Faith and Justification
17. The Redeemer
18. The Christian Life
19. Morning

20. Evening

21. Praise
22. The Cross and Comfort

23. Death and Burial
24. Eternity

25. Doxologies

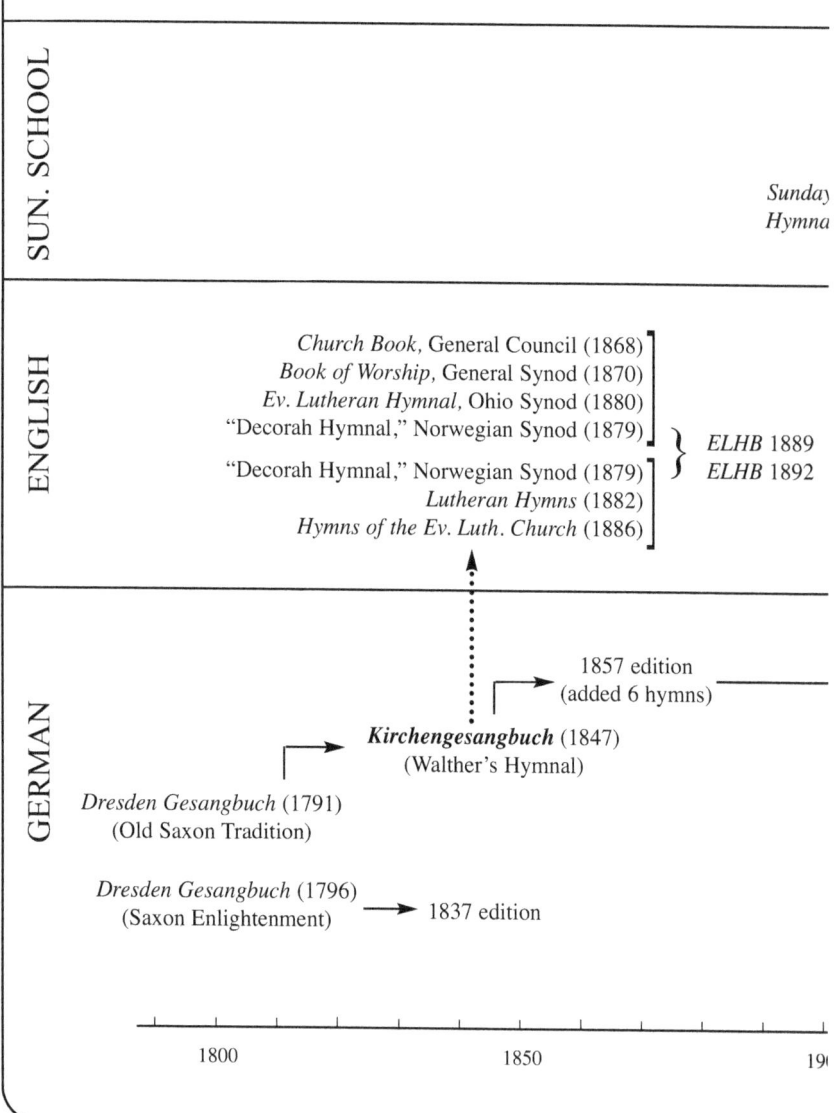

d Sunday School Hymnals

		Joyful Sounds (1977)	
y-School *il* (1901)	The Children's Hymnal (1955)	All God's People Sing! (1992)	

		Worship Supplement (1969)	Hymnal Supplement 98 (1998)
ELHB 1912 (with tunes)	**The Lutheran Hymnal** (1941)	**Lutheran Worship** (1982)	**Lutheran Service Book** (2006)

→ 1917 edition (added 41 hymns)

00　　　　　　1950　　　　　　2000

Copyright © 2012 Jon D. Vieker